An Instant Playscript

CHIMPS

SIMON BLOCK

**NICK HERN
BOOKS**

London

An Instant Playscript

Chimps first published in Great Britain in 1997
as a paperback original by Nick Hern Books Limited,
14 Larden Road, London W3 7ST

Typeset by Country Setting, Woodchurch, Kent, TN26 3TB
Printed and bound in Great Britain

ISBN 1 85459 373 0

A CIP catalogue record for this book is available from
the British Library

CHIMPS

From a few streets over
before the sun goes down
you can hear it coming closer
to this dislocated shoulder
of an old and crooked town.
That's when the ice cream van rolls around.

Ron Sexsmith

Chimps opened at the Hampstead Theatre, London, on 16 July 1997. First preview was 10 July. The cast was as follows:

STEVIE	Ashley Jensen
MARK	Darren Tighe
LAWRENCE	Nicholas Woodeson
GABRIEL	Fraser James

Directed by Gemma Bodinetz
Designed by Bruce Macadie
Lighting Designer Howard Harrison
Artistic Director Jenny Topper

ACT ONE

A KITCHEN AND FRONT ROOM OF A SMALL TERRACED HOUSE. EACH ROOM HAS ITS OWN DOOR OF ENTRY, BUT THOUGH ADJACENT THE ROOMS ARE NOT INTER-CONNECTED. THE DOOR TO THE FRONT ROOM IS OF THE STANDARD, WOOD-PANELLED VARIETY. THE DOOR TO THE KITCHEN IS OF PANELLED GLASS WITHIN A WOOD FRAME. BOTH DOORS ARE CLOSED.

EACH ROOM IS SPARSELY FURNISHED, MOSTLY WITH A FEW FAVOURED OLD PIECES, SECOND-HAND.

THE KITCHEN'S ONE OUTSTANDING FEATURE IS A LARGE ANTIQUE PINE TABLE, AROUND WHICH STAND SEVERAL MISMATCHING CHAIRS VACANTLY AWAITING THEIR FIRST GUESTS. UPSTAGE RIGHT IS A BACK-DOOR TO A GARDEN.

THE MAIN FEATURE OF THE FRONT ROOM IS A BRICKED-UP FIREPLACE IN WHICH STANDS A LARGE PHOTOGRAPH OF A YOUNG COUPLE IN A FRAMED MOMENT OF WILD DELIGHT.

PROPPED UP ON THE MANTELPIECE STAND TWO PIECES OF A2-SIZED THICK WATER-COLOUR PAPER. THE PICTURE ON THE PAPER ON THE LEFT OF THE MANTELPIECE IS A BEAUTIFULLY ACCOMPLISHED BLACK-AND-WHITE WOODCUT PRINT OF A RABBIT, WITH A LARGE, GOTHIC, LETTER – **B** – IN THE BOTTOM LEFT HAND CORNER. THE PICTURE ON THE PAPER ON THE RIGHT IS A SIMILARLY ACCOMPLISHED A BLACK-AND-WHITE WOODCUT PRINT OF AN ARMADILLO, WITH A LARGE, GOTHIC, LETTER – **A** – IN THE BOTTOM LEFT HAND CORNER. SMALL PILES OF BOOKS AND PAPERS STAND AROUND THE WALLS, AS DO SEVERAL CARDBOARD BOXES OF VARIOUS SIZES, A COUPLE OF SMALL TEA CHESTS, AND A FEW POTTED HOUSE-PLANTS OF VARIOUS SIZES. THE IMPRESSION IS OF A HOUSE RECENTLY MOVED INTO.

THE SET IS BATHED IN DAYLIGHT COMING THROUGH THE NETTED WINDOW IN THE FRONT ROOM AND THE GLASS OF THE BACK DOOR IN THE KITCHEN.

AFTER A MOMENT **MARK** AND **STEVIE** ARE SEEN THROUGH THE FRONT ROOM WINDOW APPROACHING THE UNSEEN FRONT DOOR. THEY ARE BOTH IN THEIR MID-LATE TWENTIES. **MARK** WEARS A LARGE OVERCOAT, OLD JEANS, AND WORN OUT PUMPS. **STEVIE** WEARS AN OLD *LEVI* JACKET, LOOSE-FIT TROUSERS, AND NEWER PUMPS. **STEVIE** OPENS THE DOOR WITH A KEY AND **MARK** STAGGERS THROUGH TO THE KITCHEN WITH TWO VERY HEAVILY-

LADEN BAGS OF SHOPPING FROM 'FOOD GIANT'. HE
HEAVES THE TWO BAGS ONTO THE KITCHEN TABLE.
STEVIE SAUNTERS INTO THE KITCHEN BEHIND **MARK,**
CASUALLY EATING BLACK GRAPES FROM A PUNNET.
MARK STRAIGHTENS UP AND SIGHS WITH THE EXERTION
OF HEAVING SHOPPING. **STEVIE** PICKS A GRAPE FROM THE
BUNCH AND POPS IT INTO **MARK'S** MOUTH. HE QUICKLY
EATS IT AND OPENS HIS MOUTH FOR ANOTHER. **STEVIE**
IGNORES HIM AND PEERS INTO THE SHOPPING BAGS. **MARK**
CUTS HIS LOSSES AND RETURNS TO THE FRONT DOOR AND
OUT TO THE CAR, TO FETCH THE REMAINDER OF THE
SHOPPING. **STEVIE** BEGINS TO SLOWLY UNLOAD ITEMS
FROM THE SHOPPING BAGS, ALL THE WHILE MUNCHING
GRAPES. AFTER A SHORT WHILE **MARK** RETURNS WITH
TWO MORE HEAVY SHOPPING BAGS. HE APPROACHES
STEVIE AND IS REWARDED WITH ANOTHER GRAPE
DELIVERED DIRECTLY INTO HIS MOUTH. **MARK** HEAVES
THIS SECOND PAIR OF BAGS ONTO THE KITCHEN TABLE. HE
SIGHS AGAIN. WITHOUT LOOKING AT HIM **STEVIE** OFFERS
MARK ANOTHER GRAPE. HE TAKES IT FROM HER FINGERS
AND EXITS ONCE MORE. **STEVIE** CONTINUES TO SLOWLY
UNLOAD THE SHOPPING ONTO THE TABLE. MOMENTS
LATER **MARK** RETURNS, CLOSES THE FRONT DOOR WITH
HIS FOOT, AND STAGGERS INTO THE KITCHEN WITH A
THIRD PAIR OF HEAVY SHOPPING BAGS. **STEVIE** HOLDS
OUT ANOTHER GRAPE, WHICH HE TAKES AS BEFORE. **MARK**
THEN HAULS THE FINAL PAIR OF BAGS ONTO THE TABLE.
HE LETS OUT A LARGE SIGH OF RELIEF. **STEVIE** CONTINUES
TO SLOWLY UNLOAD SHOPPING. **MARK** SURVEYS THE
TABLE.

MARK: Jesus . . .

STEVIE: What?

MARK: We're never going to eat all this.

STEVIE: Here we go . . .

MARK: How do we manage to eat all this every week?

STEVIE: Because we get hungry every day.

STEVIE HOLDS OUT A GRAPE. **MARK** TAKES IT IN HIS
MOUTH.

MARK: (Chewing) Even so.

STEVIE: Fine. Next Saturday we'll just buy a packet of crisps each.

MARK: It just seems excessive. That's all I'm saying.

STEVIE: But you say it every Saturday. And every Friday night you
start moaning how low we are on everything.

MARK NOW STARTS TO PICK UP UNPACKED SHOPPING
FROM THE TABLE AND PUT IT AWAY IN CUPBOARDS. HE
KNOWS WHERE EVERYTHING GOES, AND THIS PROCESS OF

STEVIE UNPACKING AND **MARK** PUTTING AWAY IS VERY SLICK, IF NOT PARTICULARLY HURRIED. IT CONTINUES UNTIL STATED OTHERWISE.

MARK: Maybe we're eating too much.

STEVIE: We're not eating too much . . . .

MARK: Maybe we're eating too fast.

STEVIE: (Plopping a grape in his mouth) Then chew . . . slowly.

MARK PICKS UP FOUR PACKETS OF JELLY, CROSSES TO PUT THEM AWAY, BUT STOPS HALFWAY.

MARK: Stevie, why am I putting away four packets of jelly?

STEVIE: Because we bought four packets of jelly.

MARK: Yeah, but why?

STEVIE: Because I put four packets of jelly in our trolley, and if you don't pay for them it's called stealing. Which is widely frowned upon.

MARK: Yeah . . . but why four packets?

STEVIE: I like jelly.

MARK: Since when?

STEVIE: I've always liked jelly.

MARK: Hand on my heart, I never saw you buy jelly before.

STEVIE: Yeah, you have.

MARK: Not in bulk.

STEVIE: Four isn't bulk, Mark. Bulk is four hundred.

MARK: Hey! Maybe it's your first craving!

STEVIE: If they come at all, cravings generally come much later on.

MARK: P'raps it's a pre-craving craving. P'raps your body's running a jelly test to see if there's any point craving it when the real cravings kick in.

STEVIE: All I know is I just fancied some jelly.

MARK: But you bought four – which indicates you're already planning to eat the second after the first, not to mention the third after the second and the fourth after the third. See . . . the jelly's not associated with any event, you've just got this illogical . . . *need.* Now . . . compare that to the *single* bottle of champagne I got while you were wandering round *Mothercare* . . .

STEVIE: What single bottle of champagne?

MARK: (Taking a paper-wrapped bottle of champagne from his overcoat pocket) This one.

STEVIE: When did you buy that?

MARK: I picked it up to celebrate the fantastic start to the book. (Unwrapping it and placing it on the work-top) See . . . the difference between jelly and champagne is I don't *crave* champagne for it's own sake. Just want *one* bottle *specifically* to celebrate the fantastic start to the book. The champagne and the book're related, whereas you just want jelly per se. *Ipso facto* . . . craving.

STEVIE: How much did that cost?

MARK: Not much.

STEVIE: It doesn't look a particularly cheap one, Mark.

MARK: Well . . . no point buying crap champagne, Stevie. May as well piss in tonic and cork it.

STEVIE: Given that we've got *no* spare cash at the moment . . . how much?

MARK: The thing about champagne is you get what you pay for. I've made a great start to the book Steve. Given what I've been going through since we left college I think it's worth a half decent celebration.

STEVIE: How half decent?

PAUSE.

MARK: A bit over fifteen.

STEVIE: Over fifteen? How much of a bit over?

MARK: (Beat) Twenty-five.

STEVIE: (Staggered) Forty pounds!

MARK: Actually it was only thirty-eight, so that's considerably less than you thought.

STEVIE: Only two pounds less!

MARK: It all adds up when you're on a tight budget. (Beat) Don't look at me like that, Steven. I've made a stunning start to the book!

STEVIE: You've only done 'A' is for armadillo 'B' is for bunny –

MARK: It's not simply the quantity, Steve –

STEVIE: – and I wouldn't call forty pounds on one bottle of champagne *half decent*, Mark.

MARK: It's not merely the *price* . . .

STEVIE: Forty quid on one bottle sounds pretty damn *whole* decent to me.

PAUSE.

MARK: You'll feel different after a glass or four. At thirty-eight quid it's bound to be a flavour to savour.

STEVIE: (Beat) Marky, you idiot, even if it was five hundred . . . I couldn't.

MARK: Don't be a killjoy.

STEVIE: I'm not being a killjoy. I'm being pregnant.

MARK: Yeah . . . but one glass won't hurt.

STEVIE: Foetal alcohol syndrome, remember?

MARK: You've got to have one glass, Steve. One glass for the superb start to the book.

STEVIE: Absolutely no.

MARK: Half a glass.

STEVIE: No.

MARK: A sniff. A sip. A *snip*.

STEVIE: No.

MARK: Well . . . thanks very much.

STEVIE: Don't you dare start sulking.

MARK: I'm not sulking, Steve. I'm just . . . disappointed.

STEVIE: Look . . . it's great you've started the book –

MARK: Still haven't told me what *you* think of them.

STEVIE: When you brought them down this morning you agreed I should have a bit of time to give you a considered response.

MARK: Okay okay.

STEVIE: (Beat) *Forty* pounds . . .

MARK: Thirty eight.

STEVIE: Thirty eight pounds on *champagne* –

MARK: Is excessive, I know. I *know*. (Beat) I thought thirty-eight was probably over the top when I was paying it . . . but I was so flush with making such a cracking start to the book.

STEVIE: I don't mean to be a killjoy, Marky. It's great that you've started the book. It's . . . *great*.

MARK: No, you're right. You *are* right, Steve. We haven't got the money. You can't drink. (Beat) Should've bought chocolates.

STEVIE: At least I could help you eat thirty-eight quid of chocolates.

MARK: Long as they weren't liqueurs.

STEVIE: Thirty-eight quid's-worth of chocolates, Marky. That's what I call a craving.

MARK: I got carried away. I wasn't thinking. Haven't had a reason to get carried away for ages.

STEVIE: Apart from the baby.

MARK: Yeah . . . apart from that I meant.

STEVIE: Hey. (Kisses him affectionately) Put the champagne in the fridge, have a grape, and we'll shut up about it.

MARK PUTS THE CHAMPAGNE IN THE FRIDGE.

MARK: There.

STEVIE: (Shaking her head) Thirty-eight pounds . . . !

MARK: Steven – you promised.

STEVIE: I'm sorry. *Sorry.*

STEVIE HOLDS OUT A GRAPE. **MARK** CROSSES TO HER AND TAKES IT WITH HIS MOUTH. **STEVIE** EATS ONE TOO. THEY CHEW IN SILENCE FOR A MOMENT.

STEVIE: Did you see *Mothercare*'s having a big sale?

MARK: (Starting to put shopping away again) Great . . .

STEVIE: It mightn't be a bad time to try and pick up some kind of pushchair.

MARK: If you hadn't taken so long in there I wouldn't't've been tempted to have a squint round the offy.

STEVIE: I wasn't that long.

MARK: You knew we had to get back by one fifteen.

STEVIE: We didn't *have* to.

MARK: You knew it was the agreed time.

STEVIE: If he was that keen he could've waited. We were only half an hour late.

MARK: He asked me what time'd be convenient. I just don't like messing people around.

STEVIE: Sad men in bad suits with an un-natural expertise in window sills are *not* people, Mark. Bargains for my baby come first.

MARK: Our baby. And he wasn't window sills.

STEVIE: If we wanted new window sills, and had the money for them, we'd have new window sills fitted already.

MARK: He wasn't selling window sills, Stevie. He wasn't selling anything.

STEVIE: Our window sills look fine to me. The surveyor from the building society didn't say anything about our window sills.

MARK: He wasn't window sills.

STEVIE: What was he then?

MARK: I can't remember. He was offering a . . . I dunno . . . a free estimate on something like window sills, only not window sills. Does anyone actually listen to these people?

STEVIE: Why you let them start talking in the first place, God alone knows. They don't start talking to me.

MARK: They never get the chance. You're just rude.

STEVIE: Not rude. I'm firm. You should try it.

MARK: Firm? Stevie, you slam the door in their face.

STEVIE: No I don't. I close it . . . very firmly.

10

MARK: Everyone's got a right to make a living.

STEVIE: Trawling for gullible first time buyers? There's living and there is living, Mark.

MARK: No – he said they were offering their offer to *every* home-owner in the road. Which must be true, 'cause I saw him wave to his work-mate at sixty-four. And they've been here years. Apparently – and this tells us something about the neighbours – but apparently I was the only one *on this street* who didn't take one look at his skin colour and shut the door.

STEVIE: He said that?

MARK: He said one woman even spat in his face.

STEVIE: Who?

MARK: A woman on this road, he said. He showed me her phlegm in a hanky, but refused to elaborate. 'Everyone's entitled to their prejudice', he said. Which I thought was bloody generous considering.

STEVIE: Nevertheless, Marky. Encouraging them by listening doesn't do anyone a favour.

MARK: Yeah, but it doesn't hurt to be civil.

STEVIE: I'm not saying you have to be rude –

MARK: Just *'firm'*.

STEVIE: Doorbell rings. Open door. They say: 'Fancy a duster?'. 'Can you smell the evil at your back gate?'. You say: 'Not today thanks'. Close door.

MARK: (Holding up a very large bag of Broccoli) When're we s'posed to eat all this?

STEVIE: I need it for the iron.

MARK: Wouldn't it be cheaper to suck on a park railing?

STEVIE: I'm doing everything by the book. Diet; exercise; sleep. I'm going to make the perfect baby. Like everything else it's all down to the preparation. Of which, speaking . . . you are starting the nursery today, aren't you?

MARK: (Feigning ignorance) Nursery? What nursery?

STEVIE: You promised yesterday you'd make a start this afternoon.

MARK: Well . . . if I said that then that must be what I said.

STEVIE: Of course, you also promised last Friday to make a start *last* Saturday.

MARK: Unfair! Last Saturday I was locked in the final stages of 'B' is for bunny.

STEVIE: Mark . . . whenever you want to put off starting something you always say you'll start it Saturday.

MARK: Well, this is the Saturday I meant.

STEVIE: You also said that last Saturday.

MARK: This Saturday's different.

STEVIE: Because your conviction to keep your word's stronger by seven days?

MARK: Did I say that last Saturday?

STEVIE: Just before crossing your heart and hoping to die.

MARK: Well . . . today you have my word as a former scout.

STEVIE: Don't want your word as a former scout, Mark. Just want a nursery for my baby.

MARK: Our baby. I promise. Soon as we've put this stuff away I'll make a start.

STEVIE KISSES HIM.

STEVIE: Thank you.

MARK KISSES HER.

MARK: Just give us a clue what you think about 'A' is for armadillo 'B' is for bunny.

STEVIE: Mark . . .

MARK: Give me an inkling. Give me the *tinkling* of an inkling.

STEVIE: Marky, you agreed at this point in your career, more than anything else, you need an opinion based on more than my biased enthusiasm.

MARK: Yes I know. But it's been –

STEVIE: Anything short of an objective, professional judgement at this stage would be pointless, if not criminally reckless. Now you *agreed.*

MARK: But it's been over three hours since I brought them down.

STEVIE: And over four months in the making, so don't rush me.

MARK: But they must've made a first impression.

STEVIE: And the first impression is that they look very beautiful. All your work always *looks* very beautiful.

PAUSE.

MARK: But?

PAUSE.

THROUGH THE FRONT ROOM WINDOW TWO FIGURES STEP UP TO THE FRONT DOOR.

STEVIE: It might not be a 'but'. It might simply be a 'perhaps'.

MARK: Perhaps what?

THE DOORBELL RINGS.

MARK: Pretend we're not here. Perhaps *what?*

THE DOORBELL RINGS.

STEVIE: This is why you never give them the time of day. You talk to one, he sells your name to someone else . . . you might as well put up a sign.

MARK: It might be something important.

STEVIE: On Saturday afternoon?

MARK: The estate agent with the attic keys?

STEVIE: He can stick them through the letterbox.

MARK: You know what he's like about keys.

STEVIE: (Mimicking a London wide boy) 'From my 'and to your 'and is *safe* 'ands'.

THEY GIGGLE. THE DOORBELL RINGS AGAIN.

STEVIE: Have a look through the front window. If we don't know who it is, don't answer.

MARK: Okay.

MARK CROSSES INTO THE FRONT ROOM AND SIDLES UP TO THE WINDOW. **STEVIE** FOLLOWS BEHIND AND CROUCHES BEHIND THE SOFA. **MARK** CAUTIOUSLY LOOKS THROUGH THE WINDOW.

MARK: It's the guy!

STEVIE: What guy?

MARK: The not-the-window-sill guy. Oh . . .

STEVIE: What?

MARK: There's another guy with him.

STEVIE: Who?

MARK: Another not-a-window-sill guy I guess.

STEVIE: *Two* window sill guys? How many guys does a window sill need?

THE DOORBELL RINGS AGAIN.

MARK: I should answer the door.

STEVIE: They said they'd be here at one fifteen. It's now five past two. They're late. Tough.

MARK: Maybe they came at one fifteen, found us out, and came back.

STEVIE: It's possible . . .

MARK: It's more than possible, Steve. It's probably likely.

ONE OF THE MEN IS NOW LOOKING THROUGH THE WINDOW INTO THE FRONT ROOM. HE THINKS HE SEES **MARK** AND WAVES. **MARK** FREEZES.

MARK: (Hoarse loud whisper) Shit! I think I was just spotted!

STEVIE: Shit.

THE DOORBELL RINGS AGAIN.

MARK: Shit. (Beat) I don't like to mess people round, Steve. It'll look stupid if I don't go.

STEVIE: Okay. Just tell them it's gone one-fifteen and you're busy now.

MARK: (Crossing out of the front room) Okay.

STEVIE: (Crossing out of the front room) You've got to start the nursery, and I've got to get ready.

MARK: You're not still going?

STEVIE: Why not?

MARK: But –

STEVIE: But what?

MARK: Self-defence classes aren't exactly noted for their desk-bound sessions of abstract theory.

STEVIE: I can still exercise. I can still watch.

MARK: Even so . . .

STEVIE: I do know how to take care of the baby, Mark.

MARK: Our baby.

STEVIE: Did I say it wasn't? Don't be so bossy.

MARK: I thought you wanted me to be firm.

THE DOORBELL RINGS.

STEVIE: With *them*, not me.

STEVIE EXITS. AFTER A MOMENT MARK EXITS AND OPENS THE FRONT DOOR. FOR A FEW MOMENTS A CONVERSATION TAKES PLACE AT THE FRONT DOOR, WHICH SHOULD BE VISIBLE THROUGH THE DOOR TO THE FRONT ROOM.

LAWRENCE: Hello there. We thought we might have missed you.

MARK: No, no. Look, I'm really sorry about this –

GABRIEL: We did say one fifteen.

MARK: I'm really sorry. We went shopping this morning –

LAWRENCE: Shopping. That's what I thought.

GABRIEL: We did say one fifteen?

MARK: Yes we did.

GABRIEL: I didn't get that wrong then?

MARK: No, no. We were shopping . . . the queues were unbelievable. And then we got caught in traffic coming back . . .

LAWRENCE: Traffic. That's what I thought. I knew it was traffic or something of that nature. I'm Lawrence Davidson. Very pleased to meet you. You've already met my colleague, Gabriel, of course.

MARK: Hello again. Look, I'm really sorry to do this to you – I mean . . . we were late getting back . . .

LAWRENCE: Don't apologise. Traffic happens all the time. There ought to be a law against it. There is a law against it. Unfortunately not in this country. Excuse me, but would you mind if we just stepped inside? It's somewhat nippy on the bone on your doorstep.

MARK: Inside?

LAWRENCE: In our line, in this weather, we try and snatch a little heating where we can.

MARK: Inside the house?

LAWRENCE: We can stand in this wind if you prefer. I for one am wearing thick socks and an additional pair of pants. I can't speak for Gabriel, of course . . .

GABRIEL: I dressed for early Spring I'm afraid.

PAUSE.

MARK: No, no. Well . . . okay. Come in. For a minute.

LAWRENCE: A minute's perfect. More than a minute would be over-generous. Just to melt off the chill.

LAWRENCE ENTERS THE FRONT ROOM. HE IS A MAN IN HIS MID-FIFTIES IN TWEEDS, BROGUES, AND A BARBOUR COAT. HE IS FOLLOWED BY **GABRIEL**, A SMARTLY DRESSED YOUNG BLACK MAN AGED NO MORE THAN HIS MID-THIRTIES. **MARK** CLOSES THE FRONT DOOR AND BRINGS UP THE REAR. AS THEY ENTER THE FRONT ROOM THE TWO STRANGERS QUICKLY SIZE UP THE ENVIRONMENT.

LAWRENCE: We were on our way back to the office and I said to young Gabriel, 'why don't we give Mark and Stevie one more try?'. We were stuck in traffic at the time, and I said, 'they probably got stuck in traffic'. Extraordinary how the mind works, don't you think?

MARK: I suppose so.

LAWRENCE: *Marks and Spencers*?

MARK: Sorry?

LAWRENCE: You were shopping at *Marks and Spencers,* Muswell Hill? Beautiful shop. Lovely view of north east London from the carpark.

MARK: We don't go there. It's not really . . . it's not exactly local.

LAWRENCE: I daresay it is somewhat out of your way. Do a lovely mango, *M&S*. You should treat yourself.

MARK: Maybe I will.

LAWRENCE: You should. (Beat) Well. This is what I'd call a really nice little place. Some houses you walk right up to and say, 'this is the house for me. It may need work, it may not, I don't care, I'm buying it'. Know what I mean?

MARK: Yes I do.

LAWRENCE: I could tell. (Lays a hand on his heart) And you know you made the right decision. In here.

MARK: I hope so.

LAWRENCE: Gut instinct's still worth a thousand bits of paper. And there's still no computer on this planet can tell you how you *feel*.

MARK: I agree.

GABRIEL: According to a recent finding, one in eight home-buyers don't bother with an independent survey now.

MARK: One in eight?

LAWRENCE: One in eight argue 'why should we lay out for an independent survey, when we know in our deepest gut that this is the house for us'. In our business we find people are starting to trust their own instincts again. We say good. And about time.

GABRIEL: When you boil it right down there are good surveyors and bad surveyors. It's a gamble. So one in eight are thinking 'if we don't want to lose the lottery, we won't buy a ticket'.

PAUSE.

LAWRENCE: First home?

MARK: That's right.

LAWRENCE: Spacious yet cosy. Just what you need. Plenty of potential. You really can't go wrong with these old terrace houses.

MARK: Excuse the mess.

LAWRENCE: You should see my place on a weekend.

MARK: We only moved in the day before Christmas.

LAWRENCE: Day before Christmas?

MARK: Night before, really.

LAWRENCE: Christmas eve?

MARK: Think of your worst nightmare, then double it.

LAWRENCE: I have but two words to throw into the hat. The first word is 'solicitor'. And the second word is 'conveyance'. I'd drink tea from a toilet if you to tell me I'm wrong.

MARK: I wish I could.

LAWRENCE: But you can't, 'cause those bastards are slow as slugs when it comes to other people's happiness. When they want their fee it's a blur of buttons, so fast they dial. I have a theory about solicitors. May I sit?

MARK: Sit?

LAWRENCE: As in sit *down*? If this was Portugal I'd be skipping around in lemon espadrilles, bathing trunks, and frankly little else. But in this cold, with my feet, in these shoes . . .

MARK: No. Okay. Um. Take a seat.

16

LAWRENCE: (Sitting) Ooo, that's wonderful. (Sighs) I have a theory about solicitors. And my theory about solicitors is that they are, as a rule, mentally retarded. You're not a solicitor?

MARK: I'm an illustrator.

LAWRENCE: Yes, Gabriel said. Your wife isn't –

MARK: My partner.

LAWRENCE: 'Partner'. You got to be so careful not to offend today. Partner, mistress, 'friend'. She's not a solicitor?

MARK: She's a graphic designer. Computers.

LAWRENCE: Nice. Then I can – okay. Solicitors.

GABRIEL: Mr Davidson?

LAWRENCE: The Law is what?

MARK: The law?

GABRIEL: Mr Davidson, you asked me to remind you about Mr Arnold.

LAWRENCE: Mr Arnold?

GABRIEL: Your six o'clock appointment with Mr Arnold. Tonight. At *six*.

LAWRENCE: (Beat) Right. Okay. So the difference between a solicitor and a bucket of shit is what?

GABRIEL: *Mr* Davidson?

LAWRENCE: The bucket. Am I entirely wrong? I don't think so.

MARK: My brother's a solicitor.

PAUSE.

LAWRENCE: Your brother?

MARK: Yeah.

LAWRENCE: Your brother's a solicitor?

MARK: Yeah.

LAWRENCE: (To Gabriel) His brother's a solicitor.

GABRIEL: A lot of people are.

LAWRENCE: Obviously I was exaggerating for comic effect. When I said 'the bucket' –

GABRIEL: (Pointing at the two prints) Are these an example of your work, Mark?

MARK: Uhuh. I'm creating an alphabet book for toddlers.

GABRIEL: They're exquisite.

MARK: Thanks.

GABRIEL: I've got a toddler myself, and I can honestly say I've seen nothing to touch this.

MARK: Well . . . this is my big project. The one I've been holding on for.

GABRIEL: Nothing to touch this at all.

MARK: Thanks.

GABRIEL: You work from home, if I recall?

MARK: I converted a box-room upstairs.

LAWRENCE: I expect working from home requires fantastic self-discipline.

MARK: I don't need anyone's bad breath on my shoulder for motivation, if that's what you mean.

LAWRENCE: No, no. I can see that. 'A' is for . . . what is that? Anteater?

GABRIEL: I think it's an armadillo, Mr Davidson.

MARK: 'A' is for armadillo, 'B' is for bunny. The plan is for the book to serve as a stunning calling card.

LAWRENCE: Wonderful. I used to know a song about an armadillo. I forget how it went.

GABRIEL: I expect with work of this quality you're highly sought after.

MARK: My aim isn't to fall into someone else's niche, but to create my own.

GABRIEL: And what if you don't?

MARK: I will.

GABRIEL: But what if – what if you don't?

MARK: I will.

LAWRENCE: What my partner is trying to say is, what if you don't?

MARK: (Beat) Well, then, I'll probably go back to the Post Office.

LAWRENCE: Designing stamps.

MARK: Delivering post.

GABRIEL: You delivered post?

MARK: For a couple of years. I worked out it'd take at least two years for my own style to mature. The Post Office was ideal. Mail in the morning, work at home in the afternoon. Plus, some real life experience couldn't exactly hurt.

LAWRENCE: I'm impressed.

MARK: Don't be. It didn't work out.

LAWRENCE: I'm sorry.

MARK: I resented every minute I was there, and was too knackered delivering mail to work properly. And then one morning the thought occurred to me that maybe, at heart, I'm not an illustrator at all. Maybe, at heart, I'm actually just a postman. That's when I walked out.

GABRIEL: If it's any consolation, I'd say you definitely made the right decision.

MARK: Thank you.

GABRIEL: Definitely.

LAWRENCE: Definitely.

GABRIEL: But you'll go back to the Post Office if the book doesn't work?

MARK: The book will work.

GABRIEL: Of course it will. Any fool can see that.

MARK: Thanks. Um . . . look. (Checking his watch) I don't mean to be rude –

LAWRENCE: But could we get on with it? It's later than you planned. It's Saturday afternoon. Things to do around the house, am I right?

MARK: (To Gabriel) I promised Stevie I'd make a start today.

LAWRENCE: Shelves?

MARK: (To Gabriel) She thinks I keep putting it off. Which is true, in the sense that I do.

LAWRENCE: Shelves?

MARK: What?

LAWRENCE: She wants shelves?

MARK: No.

LAWRENCE: Mine's always on at me for more shelves. Is it shelves?

MARK: No.

LAWRENCE: Lucky you. My house is flooded with shelves. Yards and yards of them. All empty. She doesn't keep books. Reads them and gives them away. But from somewhere she's got the idea shelving makes the house look classy. Personally, I feel like I'm living in 'Fahrenheit 451'. You know 'Fahrenheit 451', Mark?

MARK: I think I've heard of it.

LAWRENCE: Great book, dreadful film. Tragic if it was the other way round, given it's subject matter. So it's not shelves?

MARK: A nursery.

LAWRENCE: Oh, a nursery.

MARK: That's right.

LAWRENCE: So you're expecting?

MARK: Uhuh.

LAWRENCE: A baby?

GABRIEL: Congratulations. Your first?

MARK: Far as I know.

GABRIEL: Imminent?

MARK: Yeah, no, but –

LAWRENCE: Preparation can't start too soon. I should know, I had four. Up to a certain age children are a one of life's fundamental pleasures. Daddy this, daddy that, a kiss in the morning, a hug at bedtime. Follow you round like a string of ducklings. Then they start thinking for themselves. And then they develop a vocabulary. And then they sink in their hooks and slowly start to rip you to little, tiny pieces. A word of advice about your children: don't get too involved. Believe me when I say there's only so much bile you can swallow. Gabriel here . . . my God. How many was it last time we counted? Six? He's got six of them.

GABRIEL: Mr Davidson.

MARK: Six?

LAWRENCE: It's like a hobby with him.

GABRIEL: We really should get on.

LAWRENCE: Absolutely.

MARK: Excuse me. Before you . . . sorry.

LAWRENCE: You've a question?

MARK: Okay. I don't want you to take offence.

LAWRENCE: We're not in the taking offence business.

MARK: The free estimate.

LAWRENCE: Yes indeed.

MARK: Don't take offence, but is it? Free, I mean. Because we wouldn't. I mean. If there was some kind of outlay . . .

PAUSE.

LAWRENCE: Go on.

MARK: (Pause) Well . . . in that event we wouldn't want it.

PAUSE. **LAWRENCE** LOOKS TO **GABRIEL**, THEN TO **MARK**.

LAWRENCE: When Gabriel called last week what service did he offer?

MARK: A free estimate.

LAWRENCE: The adjective being?

MARK: Free.

LAWRENCE: By which we commonly understand there to be?

MARK: No charge.

LAWRENCE: We're not wide boys, Mark. I can assure you our company is famously narrow.

MARK: You're taking offence.

LAWRENCE: Not at all. Simply that our company prefers to leave greater width to those who knowingly or otherwise deliver a low calibre service. Those who are what we in the business call, and forgive me for being technical, 'shit'.

MARK: I've offended you.

LAWRENCE: Not me.

MARK: I'm sorry.

LAWRENCE: Do you see a ten gallon hat on my head?

MARK: No.

LAWRENCE: Do you see six-shooters at my hips?

MARK: No.

LAWRENCE: Am I wearing leather chaps?

MARK: No.

LAWRENCE: So a cowboy I'm not.

MARK: I'm sorry if I offended you.

LAWRENCE: You haven't.

MARK: I can tell.

LAWRENCE: We find this attitude all the time don't we, Gabriel?

GABRIEL: Yes we do, Mr Davidson.

MARK: What can I say except I'm sorry?

LAWRENCE: Well. Instead of 'sorry', you could say: tea.

MARK: Tea?

LAWRENCE: (Standing) Tea would be lovely. One sugar for me. Milky. Just what the doctor ordered to raise the body's core temperature.

GABRIEL: (Standing) Earl Grey if you have any. Black.

MARK: (Standing) Okay. (Beat) Okay. Well . . . I'll make tea while you . . . get on.

GABRIEL: Perfect.

MARK: Yeah. Look. I'm. Okay. Look. You just get on.

LAWRENCE: The sooner we get on the sooner we can get off and leave you to your nursery.

MARK EXITS, REAPPEARING A FEW MOMENTS LATER IN THE KITCHEN. **GABRIEL** WAITS FOR A MOMENT, THEN TURNS ON **LAWRENCE**.

GABRIEL: What's wrong with you? Six kids? It's the end of the 20th Century, Lawrence, who can afford six kids these days? Who's got the sperm count? I have one baby daughter. What's wrong with a single baby daughter?

LAWRENCE: I was building a bridge of mutual interest. After he said they've one on the way I thought the more kids we all had between us the stronger the bridge'd be. One didn't seem quite enough.

GABRIEL: One is plenty. More important: one is credible.

LAWRENCE: I'm sorry, Mr James. I thought he could swallow six kids.

GABRIEL: And that crack about solicitors.

LAWRENCE: I know. I'm sorry. I've got a thing about solicitors. When I lost the business those fucking vultures –

GABRIEL: (Cutting him off) Larry. Contrary to propaganda broadcast by the Ugly, first impressions *do* count. Within thirty seconds of entry you branded his brother mentally defective and consolidated by comparing him to a pail of excrement.

LAWRENCE: It was a calculated gamble. Which, I admit, went horribly wrong.

GABRIEL: I appreciate this is your first time solo, as it were. But you must also appreciate I can't keep stepping in. My ancillary role here is to make the final assessment of your professional aptitude, and report to Arnold with respect to your permanent employ. As you know, that report finds Arnold by six tonight.

LAWRENCE: It's just a spot of nervousness, Mr James.

GABRIEL: You're nervous, I'm nervous, our friend out there's nervous. We're all nervous 'cause none of us knows what's going to happen next. However. I'm looking for control in the midst of nerves. I'm looking for economy of thought and movement. Guts and brains, Lawrence. Get it together 'cause you're leaking all over the place, and letting the product down. Remember your training. Two words, Larry.

LAWRENCE: I know.

GABRIEL: Let's hear them.

LAWRENCE: 'Take responsibility'.

GABRIEL: So take it. You were taken on because the company's current policy is to recruit males over a certain age. Males over a certain age will accept anything to get work and most things to keep it. This is current policy. It is not, however, a religious conviction. If current policy fails the company will find a new current policy. One to which you may or may not be a party. This is one of the more simple facts of life.

LAWRENCE: For men of my age it's tougher now. No use moaning about that.

GABRIEL HOLDS UP TWO FINGERS FOR A FEW SECONDS.

GABRIEL: Two choices. (Lowers one of the fingers) You can cuddle up to your lady wife tonight with an 8% commission bulging in your trousers. Or . . . (raises the finger) . . . you cuddle up to her . . . redundant. *Again.* Glory or pity, Lawrence. It's your choice. I shall not be mentioning this again this afternoon.

PAUSE.

LAWRENCE: You know there's something about that boy reminds me of my son-in-law.

GABRIEL: You let your daughter mate with something like that?

LAWRENCE: Seems likeable enough.

GABRIEL: (Beat) Let's get to work.

LAWRENCE: Nice place they got here. Spacious yet cosy.

GABRIEL: (Holding the door open) Save it for those who need to believe it.

LAWRENCE EXITS. **GABRIEL** IS ALONE IN THE ROOM. HE LOOKS AROUND FOR A MOMENT. HE NOTICES THE FRAMED PHOTOGRAPH OF **MARK** AND **STEVIE** IN THE FIREPLACE. HE PICKS IT UP AND REGARDS IT. AFTER A MOMENT HE TAKES OUT A HANDKERCHIEF AND WIPES THE GLASS DOWN. HE THEN EXAMINES THE PHOTOGRAPH CAREFULLY BEFORE RE-SETTING IT IN THE FIREPLACE. HE TAKES A STEP BACK AND REGARDS THE PHOTOGRAPH FOR A MOMENT. HE CHECKS HIS WATCH AND QUICKLY EXITS.

MARK PUTS AWAY THE REMAINDER OF THE SHOPPING. HE WILL THEN MAKE TEA FOR THE TWO SALESMEN. **STEVIE** ENTERS IN TRACKSUIT BOTTOMS, T-SHIRT AND PUMPS.

STEVIE: Have you seen my blue sweatshirt? The one with the thing.

MARK: Try the line.

STEVIE: The line?

MARK: The washing line.

STEVIE: What's it doing there?

MARK: Hanging I expect. By the arms probably.

STEVIE: When did you wash it?

MARK: Um, Thursday.

STEVIE: It's been on the line since Thursday? Why didn't you bring it in? It rained last night.

MARK: I didn't know it was going to rain last night. I actually have little or no sway over the elements.

STEVIE: I didn't say you had sway over the elements, Mark.

MARK: Hasn't rained this morning.

STEVIE: That's not the point.

MARK: Should be dry by now.

STEVIE: That isn't the point. Rain absorbs all sorts of crap on it's way down.

MARK: Sorry, Steve. I'm trying hard to get worked up about this. But I think, basically, I don't have the strength to care.

STEVIE: (Beat) Did you send the window sills away?

MARK: Yeah, I thought about it. But then I thought 'cause we were sort of in the wrong by getting back so late –

STEVIE: We weren't in the wrong, Mark. Just late getting back.

MARK: Yeah, well, they were still up for giving us the free estimate, so I thought . . . fair do's.

STEVIE: Marky . . .

MARK: I don't like messing people around, Steve.

STEVIE: (Beat) Okay. But after these two, no more.

MARK: How long can a free estimate take?

STEVIE: No more.

MARK: Guides honour.

STEVIE CROSSES TO THE BACK DOOR, UNBOLTS IT AND EXITS. **MARK** NOW STARTS TO PREPARE TWO CUPS OF TEA. AFTER A FEW MOMENTS **STEVIE** RE-ENTERS HOLDING THE DRY SWEATSHIRT.

STEVIE: Look at this.

MARK: What am I looking at?

STEVIE: Smell it.

MARK: From here?

STEVIE: It smells.

MARK: It looks fine.

STEVIE: It looks fine but smells like crap. Smell it.

MARK: I don't want to smell it.

STEVIE: It smells like something that came out of a bird.

MARK: Like what? An egg? What?

STEVIE: Like bird pee.

MARK: (Smelling it) I can't smell anything.

STEVIE: I'm at work all day, Mark.

MARK: I know.

STEVIE: We agreed you'd do the washing.

MARK: I know.

STEVIE: Because you're here all day.

MARK: I admit it. I work from home. I can do washing.

STEVIE: And part of the washing properly is the drying properly.

MARK: Is there some way to change the subject before I die of boredom?

STEVIE: Oh, I'm sorry. I didn't realise I was *nagging* you.

24

MARK: I didn't say you were nagging me, Steve. Not nagging. *Going on* a bit, maybe . . .

STEVIE: And I'm not as bored saying it as you are hearing it? I'm only asking if you're going to do these things to please do these things properly.

MARK: Properly?

STEVIE: Properly.

MARK: Your properly.

STEVIE: My properly is simply properly, Mark.

MARK: It's an old sweatshirt, Steven. Are we seriously running this low on trivia?

PAUSE.

STEVIE: I was watching the window sills from the bedroom. They're taking photos of the front of the house.

MARK: Someone takes photos, someone draws your property in pencil. Everyone's got a gimmick.

STEVIE: Why does it need two of them to give a free estimate?

MARK: Maybe they've got a big calculator. (Spooning one teaspoon of sugar into a mug) Maybe one of them holds it while the other one pushes the buttons.

STEVIE: What are you doing?

MARK: What does it look like I'm doing?

STEVIE: You're not making tea for them?

MARK: I'm being nice.

STEVIE: They'll think you like them.

MARK: The older one's pretty entertaining actually. Doesn't know when to shut up. Poor old sod.

STEVIE: (Harsh whisper) You don't want to make them tea!

MARK: Stephen, okay. Look at me. (Beat) I'm a grown male with hair all over his body. If I want to make tea for them I will make tea for them. If I want to give them a biscuit I might even do that as well.

STEVIE: (Harsh whisper) You don't want to make them feel welcome.

MARK: *I* arranged the free estimate, so why don't you let *me* handle it. I asked them if they wanted tea and they said yes. If you really need something to disapprove of, get a dog that won't fetch.

STEVIE: If they wanted tea why didn't they bring a thermos?

MARK: Maybe they're not thermos people.

STEVIE: What's a thermos person?

MARK: Someone with a thermos.

STEVIE: I'm going to get ready.

STEVIE CROSSES TO THE KITCHEN DOOR.

MARK: They loved my pictures.

STEVIE: (Stopping) What?

MARK: They loved my pictures.

STEVIE: Who did?

MARK: They did. The window sills. They thought they were 'exquisite'.

STEVIE: So?

MARK: So it's nice to get a little support that's all.

STEVIE: I support you, Mark.

MARK: You know what I mean.

STEVIE: I haven't been paying for everything since you gave up your job? The mortgage? All our food? (Pointing to the fridge) That forty pound bottle of champagne?

MARK: Thirty-eight pounds. I'm not talking about that kind of support.

STEVIE: What kind of support are you talking about, Marky?

LAWRENCE ENTERS THE FRONT ROOM, LOOKS AROUND, THEN EXITS.

MARK: Spiritual support.

STEVIE: Spiritual support?

MARK: I need to know you're behind me on the book, Steve. Before they rang the bell you said it might not be a but, it might only be a perhaps. (Beat) Perhaps what?

LAWRENCE ENTERS THE KITCHEN.

LAWRENCE: Hello there. I'm glad you're both here 'cause you should both hear this. We've . . . um . . . found something. (Offers his hand to **STEVIE**) Lawrence Davidson.

STEVIE: (Shaking hands) Hello. And goodbye. Got to run. I'm getting ready.

LAWRENCE: I really do think you need to hear this.

MARK: She's going out.

STEVIE: Sorry.

STEVIE EXITS.

MARK: She does a self-defence class in Southgate.

LAWRENCE: Southgate? Not quite Cockfosters not quite Arkley, but at least it's not Oakwood.

MARK: What?

LAWRENCE: You're not a native North Londoner I take it.

MARK: You said there's something we should hear.

26

LAWRENCE: She does self-defence in her condition?

MARK: Steven's her own man.

LAWRENCE: My wife's exactly the same. Good for them.

MARK: Absolutely – what do we need to hear?

LAWRENCE: Ideally you should both hear it.

MARK: If she's getting ready she's getting ready.

LAWRENCE: My wife's just the same.

MARK: So you said.

LAWRENCE: If you had a word she might reconsider.

MARK: Doubtful.

LAWRENCE: She's getting ready.

MARK: You heard her.

LAWRENCE: No time.

MARK: Seems not.

LAWRENCE: That's a pity, 'cause I've got a theory about time. And my theory about time is there's less than there used to be. I'm not one of these old farts who think youth's wasted on the young, though it is. But trust me when I say my life today's little more than a blur from which it's impossible to tell the shit from the strawberry jam. And I greatly doubt it's so different for you. So when someone steps forward and suggests – with scant opportunity for personal gain – that you should listen to what he has to say, why not listen?

MARK: Short of pinning her to the wall . . .

LAWRENCE: Get her back here. It's important.

MARK: What is?

LAWRENCE: What we think you should hear.

MARK: About the sills?

LAWRENCE: *Sills*? All right. Let's just wait calmly for Gabriel with the details. Though while we're waiting there's something you should bear in mind. And what you should bear in mind is that we are the leading firm in our field.

MARK: Can't you give me a hint at least?

LAWRENCE: We're advised not to.

MARK: What've you found?

LAWRENCE: I don't want to worry you.

MARK: Then *tell* me what you've found.

PAUSE.

LAWRENCE: I could give you a clue.

MARK: I'd be grateful.

PAUSE.

LAWRENCE: Okay. Your front wall.

MARK: Is that the clue?

LAWRENCE: Bear with me. You know the wall holding up the front of your house?

MARK: What about it?

LAWRENCE: It's about to fall down.

PAUSE.

MARK: What?

LAWRENCE: Your front wall is about to fall down.

MARK: When?

LAWRENCE: We really should wait for Gabriel and the details. I can only repeat that we are the leading firm in our field. And when the leading firm in its field tells you your front wall is about to fall down, well, you'd do well to believe it.

PAUSE.

MARK: I'm sorry but I can't believe it.

LAWRENCE: You'd do well to.

PAUSE.

MARK: (Pointing at one of the mugs) I made you tea.

LAWRENCE: (Taking it) Wonderful! (He has a sip) Gorgeous!

MARK: I think you made a mistake. I only wanted a free estimate. And frankly, I didn't even want that.

LAWRENCE: The trick at this stage is not to give in to panic. (Looking through the kitchen door) Ah. Here's Gabriel now with the details. (To **MARK**) Cheer up. It may not be that bad. Details often reveal a situation to be far better than we first fear. (**GABRIEL** enters) Is it better than we first feared, Gabriel?

GABRIEL: I'm afraid it's worse, Mr Davidson.

LAWRENCE: Oh dear.

GABRIEL: Where's Stevie?

LAWRENCE: Uh, Stevie's going out.

GABRIEL: She really ought be here, Mr Davidson.

LAWRENCE: I know. Perhaps if we explain the details to Mark he can impress the urgency of the problem on her, and she'll come down.

MARK: I'm very sorry. But I can't believe what you're telling me.

LAWRENCE: Though as you can see, he's having difficulty believing it himself. You got the Polaroids?

GABRIEL HANDS **LAWRENCE** A SMALL PILE OF POLAROIDS.

28

GABRIEL: What you have to remember, Mark, is that we are the leading company in our field.

LAWRENCE: (Pulling out a chair) (To **MARK**) I think you should sit down. (Pointing to the other mug) I think there's your tea, Gabriel. Is this tea Gabriel's?

MARK: (Sitting) Yeah. What Polaroids?

LAWRENCE: Before we go into the Polaroids, I want you to appreciate that we are giving estimates –

GABRIEL: *Free* estimates.

LAWRENCE: Free estimates every day of the week. Including Sundays. That's what we do. That's our job. Okay?

MARK: I . . . okay.

LAWRENCE: The trick at this stage is to take it one step at a time.

MARK: Take what one step at a time?

LAWRENCE: Let's not get ahead of ourselves. We're taking it one step at a time, remember. I'm about to ask Gabriel to go and examine the exterior back wall of the house, while I explain the implications of our front wall examination.

MARK: It's about to fall down, you said.

GABRIEL: Is that what you said, Mr Davidson?

LAWRENCE: It was merely a *clue*. Mark was growing agitated. I simply wanted to alleviate his anxiety.

GABRIEL: I thought you'd've *preferred* to wait for the details.

LAWRENCE: Right. To the back of the house please, Gabriel. We mustn't keep young Mark on the rack a second longer than necessary.

GABRIEL REGARDS LAWRENCE FOR A MOMENT. HE RESTS A HAND FIRMLY UPON LAWRENCE'S SHOULDER, THEN EXITS THROUGH THE BACK DOOR WITH HIS TEA, THE POLAROID CAMERA AND A CLIPBOARD. PAUSE. LAWRENCE TAKES A SIP OF TEA.

LAWRENCE: Hmm. Terrific cup of tea. Thanks. Okay. (Pause) First of all. First of all . . . forget anything I might've said about your front wall being about to fall down.

MARK: Forget you said it's about to fall down?

LAWRENCE: Forget I said that.

MARK: It isn't about to fall down?

LAWRENCE: I didn't say that. Just at this moment it's not a primary concern.

MARK: It is to me.

LAWRENCE: Mark, let's not try boarding the train until we've consulted a timetable. I'm going to be frank with you. Of every ten houses we visit to give a free estimate, nine require no estimate of any sort. Nine of ten are structurally and aesthetically sound. *But*. But one in every ten –

MARK: You mean one like ours . . .

LAWRENCE: Don't jump the gun – but one like yours, requires serious and immediate attention. (He lays the first Polaroid in front of **MARK**) This is a picture of the front of your house. What do you see?

MARK: The front of my house.

LAWRENCE: Right. And what does the trained eye see?

MARK: The front of my house.

LAWRENCE: It sees a sponge.

MARK: (Looking closer) Where?

LAWRENCE: What am I talking about?

MARK: I have absolutely no idea.

LAWRENCE: I'm talking about MOISTURE – the absorption of. (He lays another Polaroid in front of **MARK**) I am talking about UNTREATED BRICKWORK. (He lays another Polaroid in front of **MARK**) I am talking about DEGENERATE POINTING. (He lays another Polaroid in front of **MARK**) I am talking about SPLITS IN MORTAR. (He lays another Polaroid in front of **MARK**) I am talking about EFFLORESCENCE.

MARK: Efflorescence?

LAWRENCE: A white powdery deposit created when DAMP draws CHEMICAL SALTS from within UNTREATED BRICKS. Upon exposure to the air these SALTS then crystallise on the brick FACIA. Or, to use the language of the layman, on the brick SURFACE. So I'm talking about efflorescence. (He lays another Polaroid before **MARK**) I'm talking about FUNGAL GROWTH. And last, but by no means least, I am talking about . . . (laying a final Polaroid before **MARK**) . . . SPALLING.

MARK: Spalling?

LAWRENCE: Appalling spalling as it's affectionately known in the trade. I take it you're unfamiliar with the term?

MARK: Yeah.

LAWRENCE: You're an illustrator, do I know illustrating terminology?

MARK: I don't know.

LAWRENCE: I know pencil, I know paper, I know what I like, I know what I know, and that's about all I know. I want you to imagine you're a brick.

MARK: Why?

LAWRENCE: Bear with me.

MARK: Okay.

LAWRENCE: You are a brick.

MARK: How big?

LAWRENCE: Average. Nondescript. Run of the mill.

MARK: Red?

LAWRENCE: Let's say, why not. You're an ordinary red brick mortared into the bottom of . . . (pointing at Polaroid number one) . . . the wall holding up the front of your house.

MARK: Okay.

LAWRENCE: Now, you are, and this is important – this is fundamental to the point I'm about to make – you are untreated with any SILICON-BASED WATER-REPELLENT COATING of any kind.

MARK: I'm untreated.

LAWRENCE: In brick terms you're in the buff. Naked, and consequently, for a brick, vulnerable. I'm taking it deliberately slowly so you'll have no trouble keeping up.

MARK: I'm not an idiot.

LAWRENCE: I can hear that. And frankly it makes my job a great deal easier. So picture it. You're a brick surrounded by mortar.

MARK: Okay.

LAWRENCE: On all sides. And mortar's intentionally weaker than brick.

MARK: I s'pose it would be.

LAWRENCE: Why?

MARK: Never really thought about it.

LAWRENCE: Why should you? Do I think about illustrating? Why would I?

MARK: You wouldn't.

LAWRENCE: It'd be entirely out of character if I did. Mortar's intentionally weaker than brick so it can offer less resistance – in the event of stress on the wall from movement within or *beneath* the wall foundation. I am talking now about SOIL SETTLEMENT.

MARK: Okay.

LAWRENCE: So mortar's a form of SHOCK ABSORBER soaking up the occasional movement. A slip here, a slide there. Mortar, Mark, absorbs it all.

MARK: Thank God for mortar.

LAWRENCE: Why not? So you're this brick.

MARK: Untreated, at the bottom of the wall.

LAWRENCE: Good. And you're surrounded by mortar which is soaking up WATER and SHOCK and . . . ?

MARK: And?

LAWRENCE: And CONSTANT PRESSURE from above. Constant and *tremendous* pressure from above.

MARK: The other bricks bearing down on me.

LAWRENCE: *Very* good. My job's so much easier when I'm dealing with the intelligent and articulate. Wherever you are in London it's said you're never more than seven feet from a rat. I find the same could be true for stupid people. And I'm not talking about those feeble-minded with pieces of head missing. I'm talking about people you pass in the street without a second glance. People with Koi carp in the garden, and separate bicycle insurance, and neat haircuts, and shiny shoes. The stupidity walking over your average pavement, it's a mystery how we ever made it down from the trees and stopped swinging for a living. I usually have to explain brick degeneration four or five times before the penny drops. And chances are even then the penny's not going to be particularly shiny. I'm only saying it's a pleasure talking to you.

MARK: Thanks.

LAWRENCE: A pleasure and a relief.

MARK: I don't think people think as much as they can. Maybe they can't. Maybe they don't know where to start. Television –

LAWRENCE: Television? Don't get me started on television.

MARK: I think it should only be available on prescription.

LAWRENCE: I have a theory about television and my theory is the moment they cancelled 'The Good Old Days' family entertainment lay face down dead in the water. Wholesome amusement used to be a byword. Me and my wife never missed a programme. We'd sit on our sofa, my wife with a feather boa draped across her – won't bore you with the details. Me with my comic copper's helmet – I'm straying from my point. (Beat) The point is you're a brick at the bottom of this wall. Over a given period you're subject to a variety of tremendous forces. Consequently, you begin to assume the consistency, in brick terms, of a moist biscuit. And so, eventually, *inevitably*, you start to SPALL.

GABRIEL APPEARS AT THE BACK DOOR. UNSEEN BY **MARK**, **LAWRENCE** SEES HIM AND RAISES ONE FINGER. **GABRIEL** IMMEDIATELY MOVES OUT OF SIGHT.

LAWRENCE: This is what's happening at the base of your front wall, Mark. Being untreated the wall absorbs moisture through both brick and mortar. The wall is thus DAMP, and the sheer weight of the wall under what is known in the business as GRAVITY, is causing the bricks at the wall base to lose INTERNAL STRUCTURE and, almost imperceptibly, disintegrate. Once disintegration is complete, well. I take it you're familiar with the story of Joshua and the walls of Jericho?

MARK: Yes.

LAWRENCE: You imagine for one second those walls would've collapsed like that if they'd been coated with a silicon-based water-repellent? Trumpets? Trumpet my arse. *Spalling*, Mark. Spalling brought down the walls of Jericho. Ask anyone in the building trade.

PAUSE. **GABRIEL** HAS RE-APPEARED AT THE BACK DOOR.
LAWRENCE SEES HIM AND NODS SLIGHTLY. **GABRIEL**
ENTERS.

MARK: I don't know what to say.

LAWRENCE: I know you don't. But don't worry. We've seen this
reaction a hundred times.

MARK: I really don't know what to say.

LAWRENCE: (To **GABRIEL**) What did you discover at the rear?

GABRIEL PUTS THE POLAROID CAMERA ON THE TABLE.

MARK: Not more bloody Polaroids . . .

GABRIEL: Just one more, Mark. This is the last one.

GABRIEL THEATRICALLY LAYS ONE FINAL POLAROID IN
FRONT OF **MARK** ON THE TABLE. **MARK** PICKS IT UP AND
REGARDS IT.

MARK: There's nothing there.

GABRIEL: I've just taken it.

THEY ALL WAIT FOR THE POLAROID TO DEVELOP. PAUSE.
AFTER TEN OR SO SECONDS THE POLAROID DEVELOPS.
THEY ALL LEAN CLOSER TO LOOK. PAUSE. **LAWRENCE**
THEATRICALLY POINTS TO THREE AREAS ON THE
POLAROID.

LAWRENCE: I'm afraid that speaks for itself.

GABRIEL: I really believe Stevie would want to see these. Before we
proceed any further she *needs* to see these.

GABRIEL GATHERS THE POLAROIDS TOGETHER AND
OFFERS THEM TO **MARK**.

LAWRENCE: I'm afraid it looks bad, Mark. Very bad indeed. But
nevertheless it's no cause for despair. It'd be sadistic of us to pinpoint a
problem if we couldn't, quite literally, supply the solution.

MARK: (Looking at the photos) Jesus. If this is true –

GABRIEL: Oh, it's true, Mark. Be in absolutely no doubt about that.

MARK: You go about your business assuming everything's more or
less okay. Shit. I mean . . . *shit*.

GABRIEL: Because everything seems okay don't make the mistake
that everything is. Generally speaking things are okay until we discover
that they are, in reality, the opposite. It's a forgivable error of
judgement. What is however, *unforgivable*, is the failure to act on
recognition of that error. Once Stevie sees these pictures she'll be glad
she had, and we can proceed to sort this out.

MARK: But you've only been here five minutes. How can you
possibly see all this in five minutes?

LAWRENCE: Trust me. The expert eye sees more in five minutes
than the inexpert will see in a lifetime.

PAUSE.

MARK: I don't know what to say.

GABRIEL: May I suggest nobody says anything until we've brought Stevie in here?

MARK: Okay.

GABRIEL: Lovely cup of tea, by the way.

MARK: (Weakly) Thanks.

GABRIEL: Go get Stevie, Mark.

MARK TAKES THE POLAROIDS. HE STANDS AND, AFTER A MOMENT, EXITS THE KITCHEN. **LAWRENCE** AND **GABRIEL** WATCH HIM GO. PAUSE.

GABRIEL: Keep going, Lawrence. Keep what your life needs to the fore, and you can't go wrong.

LAWRENCE: He does remind me of my son-in-law.

GABRIEL: Three words, Larry.

LAWRENCE: 'Uncertainty creates opportunity'.

GABRIEL: And what's opportunity doing at this *precise* moment?

LAWRENCE: Knocking, Mr James.

GABRIEL: You clear away. I'll get the cases.

GABRIEL EXITS THE KITCHEN. **LAWRENCE** QUICKLY CLEARS THE CHAIRS TO ONE SIDE OF THE KITCHEN, AND SETS THE TABLE UPSTAGE. HE THEN PICKS UP HIS MUG OF TEA AND TAKES A SWIG. IT IS COLD, AND HE SPITS IT BACK INTO THE MUG. HE THEN SETS THE MUG BY THE SINK AND EXITS TO THE FRONT DOOR.

STEVIE ENTERS THE FRONT ROOM, FOLLOWED BY **MARK** IMMEDIATELY BEHIND. SHE CARRIES A SPORTS HOLDALL AND A PAIR OF LACE-UP TRAINING SHOES. SHE SITS, AND STARTS TO PUT THE SHOES ON. **MARK** HOLDS OUT THE POLAROIDS.

STEVIE: Will you please stop waving those things in my face.

MARK: I'm only saying you should at least look at them.

STEVIE: This house cannot, repeat cannot, repeat cannot, repeat CANNOT be about to fall down. It's just, that's just ridiculous. I mean, who are these people, Mark? I'll tell you who they are. They're nobody.

MARK: I didn't say the house. I said the walls, front and back.

STEVIE: Just tell them to go.

MARK: Look at the Polaroids. (He tosses the Polaroids at her feet) They told me nine out of ten times they simply walk away. Nine out of ten houses are structurally and aesthetically sound.

STEVIE: What do they want to *sell* us?

34

MARK: Look at the Polaroids.

STEVIE: No, what do they want to sell us, Mark? They're salesmen. So what are they selling?

MARK: I know they're salesmen, Stevie.

STEVIE: They . . . make . . . stuff . . . up.

MARK: Yes I know. But what if this time they're not. They can't always be making stuff up. They can't always be lying. What if, okay, nine out of ten salesmen who come to our door *are* liars? But not these two.

STEVIE: By being two instead of one they haven't lied already?

MARK: No, that was me. I was under the impression there'd be just one. (Picking up a Polaroid and looking at it) Our walls look like shit.

STEVIE: Our walls are no worse than walls of their age.

MARK: You know nothing about walls.

STEVIE: I know a wall when I see one.

MARK: And I know a crack when it's highlighted. I know bad pointing when it's pointed out to me. I know spalling when someone takes the trouble to explain what spalling is?

STEVIE: Spalling?

MARK: Appalling spalling.

STEVIE: Never heard of it.

MARK: What – so it doesn't exist?

STEVIE: The walls are *fine*.

MARK: You don't know that.

STEVIE: They're fine. Of course they're fine. They were fine before they came and they'll be fine when they've gone. Which will be any second now.

LAWRENCE NOW ENTERS THE KITCHEN BEARING TWO DISPLAY BOXES, ONE LARGER THAN THE OTHER. HE SETS THEM ON THE TABLE. **GABRIEL** FOLLOWS BEHIND WITH A PORTABLE DISPLAY BOARD, WHICH HE QUICKLY SETS UP. HE THEN EXITS WITH A CLIPBOARD THROUGH THE BACK DOOR.

MARK: Yes, no, but you don't *know*. Why can't you admit that you do not actually know? Why do you always have to have the definitive opinion? You never used to be like this. At college –

STEVIE: We haven't been at college for nearly *four* years –

MARK: At college we passionately believed in having no convictions about anything. But the day you got a salary suddenly there's not a puzzle on the planet you didn't have the answer to. All of a sudden you've got knowledge with a capital N.

STEVIE: I don't know anything, Marky . . .

MARK: And notice I said knowledge, not wisdom.

STEVIE: . . . except what I pick up on the way. And what I'm told – when people choose to tell me *anything*.

MARK: What's that s'posed to mean?

STEVIE: Oh, you know exactly what I mean. There are times – and this one of them – when your little-boy-baffled routine is a fantastic pain in my arse.

MARK: I don't know what you mean. I'm sorry if I don't always immediately know what you mean.

STEVIE: I mean . . . okay. You want to carry on doing it, o.k. I mean the surprise champagne we can't actually afford. I mean the job you chuck without consulting me.

MARK: No. I consulted you, Stevie.

STEVIE: Mark, you *consulted* me a week after you gave in your notice.

MARK: I didn't want you to worry.

STEVIE: You didn't stop me worrying – just delayed it a week. And I also mean the job offer from Angelo you turned down.

PAUSE.

MARK: What job offer?

STEVIE: *Please*, Marky . . .

MARK: Angelo told you about that?

STEVIE: Grow up, Mark. I was friends with Angelo long before you. 'Course he told me. I didn't say anything because Angelo said you'd said he wasn't to say anything. And you tell him I told you he told me, I'll break one of your important bones.

MARK: They're all important.

STEVIE: For God's sake . . .

MARK: Did Angelo tell you what the job was?

STEVIE: He told me you turned it down flat.

MARK: Did he tell you what it was?

STEVIE: I don't care what it was. I care about not being told it was even offered. I care about bottles of champagne turning up from nowhere. I care about you doing all this stuff without talking it over with me.

MARK: So now I'm talking over the walls.

STEVIE: For the last time, Mark, there is nothing wrong with our walls.

MARK: Okay. Let's say you're right.

STEVIE: Let's say I am because I am.

MARK: Okay let's say that.

STEVIE: Let's.

MARK: You're right.

STEVIE: I know.

MARK: Let's say those two are fibbing all the way to the bank.

STEVIE: Which they are.

MARK: Okay. Let's say they are, and I kick them out, and we bolt the door, and our house falls down the day after tomorrow. What then?

PAUSE. **LAWRENCE** LOOKS AT HIS WATCH, THEN LEAVES THE KITCHEN THROUGH THE KITCHEN DOOR.

STEVIE: They don't know the walls will fall down.

MARK: Maybe not. But we don't know for sure they'll stay up. Do we? You know we don't.

STEVIE: Marky . . .

MARK: You know we don't , Steven.

STEVIE: Just tell them to go!

MARK: Because we never had a survey.

PAUSE.

STEVIE: We had the building society survey.

MARK: For the building society. Not for us. He tapped the staircase, jumped on a floorboard, and shook our hands.

STEVIE: He examined the walls.

MARK: No, Stevie. He glanced at them on his way out.

STEVIE: Everything happened so quickly. Mr Martin wanted a quick sale before Christmas, and we were desperate to get out of the flat.

MARK: We should've had a proper survey.

STEVIE: But we took one look at the house and we just *knew*. We just *knew*, Marky.

MARK: We'd just found out you were pregnant. You saw kids playing in every room.

STEVIE: And you were convinced this place'd give you space to grow your book.

MARK: Gut reaction.

STEVIE: We just knew.

PAUSE.

STEVIE: The survey money just about met the cost of materials for the nursery.

PAUSE. **STEVIE** BENDS AND PICKS UP THE POLAROIDS THAT HAVE BEEN LYING AT HER FEET. SHE SLOWLY SIFTS THROUGH THEM.

MARK: Shouldn't we should at least listen to what they've got to say?

STEVIE: No. (Beat) (She looks closely at one Polaroid) I don't know.

LAWRENCE OPENS THE DOOR.

LAWRENCE: So . . . Stevie. What do we think of the snaps?

STEVIE: Very nice. Did you use a tripod?

LAWRENCE: I know what you're thinking. You're thinking this is a personal judgement against you and your house – with all its associations of the HOME and such forth. You're thinking 'they probably think I'm a slut'.

STEVIE: I beg your pardon?

LAWRENCE: But let me assure you even if you were a slut, my company's not in the judgement business. Once you realise we're all pulling in the same direction –

MARK: Could we have a moment?

LAWRENCE: Alone?

MARK: Yeah.

LAWRENCE: With me or her? Only you weren't pointing at either of us.

MARK POINTS AT **STEVIE**.

LAWRENCE: Of course. We're all set up in the kitchen when you're ready.

LAWRENCE EXITS AND RETURNS TO THE KITCHEN.

STEVIE: They come into my house –

MARK: Our house, Stevie.

STEVIE: Bringing it into my home on a Saturday, after I've been working all week to keep us on the . . . and we have a right not to be . . . I mean, you never expected it at the flat. The flat was council . . . no man's land for these people. But this is ours, and I know that's why they're here, but *this* . . . this is . . . these four walls, Marky . . . this is our first *place* . . .

MARK TRIES PUTTING HIS ARMS ROUND HER.

STEVIE: Leave me alone, I'm fine. I'll be fine.

MARK: Why don't we find out what's wrong with the house and tell them to go. We're not buying anything, so why don't we take their free information then show them the door.

STEVIE: I've been looking forward to self-defence all week.

MARK: All we're be doing taking advantage of the situation. Mopping up free expertise and in all probability saving ourselves future expense.

STEVIE: We should get an independent survey.

MARK: How? We're over our hair in mortgage, Steve.

STEVIE: If you'd've taken Angelo's job we could afford a survey.

MARK: I'm an illustrator, not a typesetter.

38

STEVIE: He wanted to bring you in at the bottom.

MARK: You want someone to set type, get a typesetter. I illustrate. I was top of the year at college, in case you forgot. I won every scholarship and bursary going.

STEVIE: It was just a rung.

MARK: Typesetting on a TV listings magazine. Fuck, Steven, does it get any lower?

STEVIE: It was just the first rung.

MARK: (With a re-newed urgency) We'd be stupid not to at least listen to what they found. After all, they are the leading firm in their field.

STEVIE: You believe that?

MARK: You can't go round saying you're the leading firm in your field if you're not. You've got to draw the line somewhere. We'll play it stupid so they don't catch on it's *us* milking *them*. It'll be perfect! Fuckers! Then you can go to your class and I can get on with the nursery! (At the door) I'll ask them to speak slowly. I'll take notes with a crayon!

STEVIE: Don't over-do it.

MARK: You're right. I'll use a 3B pencil.

MARK EXITS. **STEVIE** REMAINS, COMPOSING HERSELF.

LAWRENCE AND **GABRIEL** HAVE NOW SET UP THE KITCHEN IN PREPARATION FOR THE PITCH. THIS INCLUDES A FLIP CHART WITH SEVERAL LAMINATED SHEETS AND TWO BLACK, LEATHER-FINISHED RECTANGULAR BOXES, ONE SMALLER THAN THE OTHER, EACH FITTED WITH A GOLD CLASP. HAVING SET UP THE PITCH **LAWRENCE** HAS MADE FOUR CUPS OF TEA – REQUIRING HIM TO SEARCH THROUGH FRIDGE, CUPBOARDS AND DRAWERS FOR THE RELEVANT CONSTITUENTS. **GABRIEL** HAS BEEN AT THE BACK OF THE HOUSE, HAVING BEEN AT THE FRONT FOR A SHORT WHILE MAKING NOTES ON A CLIPBOARD. HE NOW RETURNS INTO THE KITCHEN THROUGH THE BACK DOOR, HOLDING HIS CLIPBOARD, WHICH HE PUTS ON THE TABLE.

GABRIEL: The Rock Box and the Box of Tricks should swap round. Faith before fact, Lawrence.

LAWRENCE SWAPS THE BOXES OVER.

GABRIEL: They ready?

LAWRENCE: I think she's a little pissed off.

GABRIEL: Of course. We just shat in her hearth. She brings the tears, we bring the tissue.

LAWRENCE: Perhaps we should ease back a tad.

GABRIEL: ABC, Larry: 'always be closing'. Eliminate emotion. Act against feelings. Keep yourself on the edge of your seat and never lose touch with what comes out your mouth.

LAWRENCE: I thought perhaps it might be a better move at this stage to ease back. Just a tad. I only meant a tad. A tad's barely anything at all. It's scarcely a notch.

GABRIEL: Sympathy for the client is cancer of the blood in this business. The work you did before you hit the bottom and found your way to us? You were some kind of butcher, am I right?

LAWRENCE: Poulterer. I was in chickens.

GABRIEL: But meat in its dead state was involved.

LAWRENCE: What else?

GABRIEL: And to assist those birds into the hereafter you were called upon to kill.

LAWRENCE: For a gizzard to become a giblet something's got to kick the bucket. I held the bucket, Mr James, and I made sure they kicked it.

GABRIEL: For which you have an instinct.

LAWRENCE: I wouldn't call it an instinct as such.

GABRIEL: A killer instinct.

LAWRENCE: Chickens always annoyed me. Don't ask me why. It was a useful motivator.

GABRIEL: But when the job had to be done, and you were called on to do it, you didn't flinch.

LAWRENCE: I'm not a flincher.

GABRIEL: At the end of the day that's what I'm here to assess.

LAWRENCE: I never once flinched.

GABRIEL: Good for you. Because there is what there is, and we get what we deserve.

LAWRENCE: I never used to think it was that simple . . .

GABRIEL: I drive a prestige car with power steering, ABS brakes and twin airbags. I don't expect favours on the road and I don't give any. It's a crude philosophy. But it's the only one I've found that puts bread on my child's plate and keeps me on an even keel. Simplicity is the key.

PAUSE. **LAWRENCE** PICKS UP THE CLIPBOARD, AND LOOKS AT WHAT IS THERE.

LAWRENCE: You don't think this is a little overwhelming?

GABRIEL: Subtlety is for those with time to appreciate it. (He sees something through the door) Okay. Here she comes. Remember, we're telling, not selling.

LAWRENCE QUICKLY CROSSES BACK TO THE TEA THINGS AS **STEVIE** ENTERS THE KITCHEN.

LAWRENCE: I took the liberty of making us all a nice cup of tea.

STEVIE: (Flatly) I see you found everything.

40

LAWRENCE: (Offers mug) 'Seek and ye shall find', said the Bishop to the actress. 'Keep it to yourself and ye shall go blind', said the actress in reply.

STEVIE: Mark's just coming down.

LAWRENCE: We hear congratulations are in order. You look, as they say, radiant. Doesn't she look radiant, Gabriel?

GABRIEL: She does, Mr D.

STEVIE: Radiance, if it comes at all, comes much later.

LAWRENCE: Excuse me, Stevie. This may be inappropriate.

STEVIE: What?

LAWRENCE: It's about the baby.

STEVIE: What about it?

LAWRENCE: I was simply interested to know – you see, my own daughter – I was interested to know whether whether you ever considered having an abortion?

PAUSE. **MARK** ENTERS WITH A NOTEPAD AND PENCIL.

MARK: No problem if I take notes?

STEVIE: He just asked if we considered having an abortion.

MARK: What?

GABRIEL: It's really none of our business.

MARK: Yeah, I'll go along with that.

LAWRENCE: Only my daughter had one recently. Says she doesn't want to bring children into this world. But you obviously do.

MARK: I mean, what kind of question is that exactly?

LAWRENCE: I have this theory about my daughter's abortion.

GABRIEL: Mr Davidson . . .

LAWRENCE: And my theory is that she's punishing me.

STEVIE: What for?

GABRIEL: By all means take notes, Mark. Mr Davidson, the *sketches*.

GABRIEL SITS AT THE TABLE. PAUSE.

GABRIEL: Mr Davidson? The sketches?

LAWRENCE: (Beat) Right. Yes. So you've both now seen the Polaroids?

MARK: (Sitting) Yeah.

LAWRENCE: And how do you think they look?

MARK: We don't know what to think, do we, Stevie?

STEVIE: No we don't. Though we probably think they look pretty bad.

LAWRENCE: The exterior of your house has suffered years of neglect. You can see where the previous owner tried covering it up with a slap of cheap paint.

MARK: I don't think Mr Martin would've done that. He was a nice old bloke.

LAWRENCE: Pardon me, but he's selling his house for as much as he can get on the open market. Behind the dentures and cataracts was a wolf in a lambswool cardigan.

MARK: No, we also spoke to the next door neighbours to be on the safe side.

LAWRENCE: Oh, you spoke to the next door neighbours to be on the safe side?

MARK: And they said to the best of their knowledge everything was hunky dory.

LAWRENCE: Hunky dory?

MARK: That's what they said.

LAWRENCE: And you trust people for whom hunky dory's an everyday expression, do you? How long was the previous owner the previous owner?

MARK: Um, twenty three years.

LAWRENCE: Mark. Stevie. It wouldn't be the first time the neighbours came in for a slice of pie, if you catch my drift.

GABRIEL: You'd be staggered what goes on. The statistics are very revealing.

LAWRENCE: Forget the previous owner, forget the neighbours – liars all, and welcome to their ill gotten gains. Let's talk about NOW. Time takes its toll . . . water creeps into cracks . . . frost bites . . . expansion . . . splitting. That we've survived this far's a mystery to anyone who comprehends the full force of nature. (He offers the clipboard to **STEVIE**) This is a simplified pictogram of the front and back of your house. It depicts – in picture form – the main problem areas. Blue is good. Red is bad.

PAUSE.

MARK: It's all red.

LAWRENCE: Please. Let's not shoot the messenger.

GABRIEL: Admittedly we are the bearers of bad news. But we do have the means to make our borne bad news bearable.

GABRIEL SMILES ENGAGINGLY. PAUSE. **MARK** TAKES NOTES.

LAWRENCE: You got all that?

MARK: I think so.

LAWRENCE: Your walls have a problem. We quite literally have the solution.(He flips over the first page of the flip-chart) 'EX-COTE'.

(The page simply says in big, bold letters: 'EX-COTE'). Ex-Cote is a unique and outstanding wall-covering which, when applied to the walls of your home, prevents moisture from entering the wall while SIMULTANEOUSLY allowing your walls to breathe as nature intended. (To **MARK**) I can always slow down. So. From where does the magical material that is Ex-Cote come from? Is it . . . (flips over next page to reveal a picture of earth) . . . from the ground? (Flips over next page to reveal a picture of earth with a large cross superimposed over it). No. Is it . . . (flips over next page to reveal a picture of the sea) . . . from the sea? (flips over next page to reveal a picture of the sea with a large cross superimposed over it) No. Is it . . . (flips over next page to reveal a picture of the sky) . . . from the sky?

STEVIE: No.

LAWRENCE: (He flips over next page to reveal a picture of the sky with a large cross superimposed over it) Or is it from . . . (flips over next page to reveal a brochure-quality photographic still of a medium-sized industrial manufacturing plant in a sunny climate) . . . our factory in Gustavo A. Madero, formerly Guadeloupe Hidalgo, in South Central Mexico, slightly north west of Mexico City?

PAUSE.

MARK: Yes?

LAWRENCE: Is the correct answer. (He flips over next page to reveal a picture of the still with large tick superimposed over the top) Ex-Cote has been manufactured in the heart of the Mexican industrial belt for the past decade. And from here it has established itself as the number one silicon-based water repellent wall covering in the United States of America. I can tell what you're thinking.

MARK: You can?

LAWRENCE FLIPS OVER THE NEXT PAGE, WHICH IS A PICTURE OF A COW STANDING IN THE DISTANCE, WITH A COW PAT IN THE FOREGROUND.

LAWRENCE: You're thinking, bullshit.

MARK: Isn't that a cow?

LAWRENCE: Companies who endorse Ex-Cote silicon-based water-repellent wall covering:

LAWRENCE FLIPS OVER THE NEXT PAGE TO REVEAL A LIST RUNNING TO SEVERAL CLOSELY TYPED COLUMNS OF COMPANY NAMES. THE LIST IS HEADED IN LARGE, BOLD LETTERS: 'COMPANIES WHO ENDORSE EX-COTE SILICON-BASED WATER-REPELLENT WALL COVERING'.

MARK: We can read.

LAWRENCE: Simply saving you the effort.

MARK: It's no effort.

STEVIE: I have a question.

LAWRENCE: Please bear with me. (Referring to the list) Here we see leading manufacturers from the computing industry, leading petrochemical corporations, fast food chains, government agencies. The list of endorsees is, to coin a phrase, endless.

GABRIEL: Not quite endless. But the point is made.

MARK: You're big.

GABRIEL: Big and completely legitimate.

LAWRENCE: Legitimate and Global. We're a global company expanding across the – why be modest – the globe.

STEVIE: I've got a question.

LAWRENCE: Bear with me. On the back of our success in north American and European industry, we've been able to offer the protection of Ex-Cote to the private home-owner. With stunning success.

LAWRENCE FLIPS OVER THE NEXT PAGE, WHICH IS ONE OF HAND-WRITTEN ENDORSEMENTS AND PHOTOS FROM SATISFIED PRIVATE HOME-OWNERS.

MARK: They look happy.

GABRIEL: They look happy because they have what we all seek.

MARK: Ex-Cote.

GABRIEL: Peace of mind. They protected their family home.

STEVIE: Um, I've got a question.

LAWRENCE: Please. I'm asking you to please bear with me.

STEVIE: But I have a class to get to and I don't have much time.

LAWRENCE: (Smiling engagingly) The women always want to jump the gun.

STEVIE: I've got to be somewhere, and I've got a question. How much?

LONG PAUSE.

LAWRENCE: Pardon me?

STEVIE: How much?

LAWRENCE: How much?

STEVIE: How much?

LAWRENCE: In what sense?

STEVIE: In a financial sense. How much does it cost?

GABRIEL: How much does it cost?

STEVIE: I'm going to speak very slowly. (Pause) How much *money* does it cost?

LAWRENCE: The women always want to discuss price before they appreciate the value of the purchase. There's a mutually beneficial procedure operating here, Stevie. An established order of doing things. Established for a reason – the reason being that it's right. Mark appreciates this, don't you, Mark?

MARK: (Pacifying) I think we should just do what we said we'd do, Stevie. Listen carefully. Make notes. Find out what's wrong –

STEVIE: We've found out what's wrong, so –

MARK: So let's find out how to put it right. (Sotto) I mean if they're *offering* to tell us.

GABRIEL: Which we are.

STEVIE: Yes I know but –

GABRIEL: Procedure shouldn't be rushed, Stevie. Time must be invested for quality to be achieved. As an artist I know Mark appreciates this.

MARK: Absolutely.

STEVIE: Why won't you just tell us how much it costs?

LAWRENCE: I hope you're not suggesting we're deliberately holding back.

STEVIE: You are deliberately holding back.

LAWRENCE: Yes, but with very good reason.

STEVIE: I'm sorry but I'm in a hurry. Let's get to the nitty gritty and get this over with. In your opinion, how much will it cost to have our walls fixed?

LAWRENCE: Before I can answer that we have to sort the nitty from the gritty. What is nitty? What is gritty? These are complex issues.

GABRIEL: You understand the situation, Mark. I'm sure an impatient, hasty approach would be just as counter-productive in your line of work.

STEVIE: I also have a line of work.

MARK: Steve, we agreed we'd hear what they had to say.

STEVIE: I'm due at self-defence and they don't seem any closer to leaving and I've got listen this crap about 'quality' and 'artists'? What's going on here?

GABRIEL: You invited us to your home and we've come in good faith. If it hasn't yet sunk in your house is very close to catastrophic collapse.

STEVIE: *I* didn't invite you anywhere.

MARK: Stevie, we've got a plan. So let's stick to it.

GABRIEL: I'm sorry, Miss, but we haven't entered under false pretences. We're not double glazing. We're not a conservatory. We're not some fish restaurant offering free French fries. We are trained professionals with a professional responsibility in light of what we've found here this afternoon. However much you castigate us for our sense of duty we nevertheless take it extremely seriously. Now, Mark responded to my offer on your doorstep –

STEVIE: No he didn't.

MARK: Given that you want this over as soon as possible why are you dragging it out like this?

STEVIE: I'm sorry. But this stranger comes into my house evading my questions –

MARK: Our house.

STEVIE: Wouldn't you like to know exactly what Mark responded to on the doorstep?

MARK: (Overlapping) What's in those, um, cases? They look very interesting.

STEVIE: Because it certainly wasn't your *offer*, my friend.

MARK: Can we see what's in these cases?

GABRIEL: (Opens the box) In here we have the seven chief ingredients of Ex-Cote. Mr D?

LAWRENCE: (Pointing to each of seven differently coloured vials in turn) Epoxy resin, stabiliser, solvent, pigment –

STEVIE: Unless an integral part of your offer includes the colour of your skin?

PAUSE.

MARK: Stevie, shut up.

STEVIE: Mark took pity on you because you're black.

PAUSE.

MARK: (To Gabriel) I absolutely said no such thing.

STEVIE: He didn't even know what you were selling until twenty minutes ago.

MARK: For fuck's sake Stevie!

PAUSE.

GABRIEL: Go on, Mr Davidson.

LAWRENCE: (Beat) Aggregate, waterproofing, and assorted chemicals.

MARK: You stupid . . . what did you have to say that for?

STEVIE: It's true, isn't it? Why should *we* be the only ones who 'really need to know' something?

GABRIEL: (Standing) Mr Davidson, I think Mark and Stevie require a minute or two alone.

LAWRENCE: But I haven't demonstrated the unique protective nature of Ex-Cote by –

GABRIEL: (Firmly)Mr *D*.

LAWRENCE: (Rising) (Tapping the second box) Trust me. It's quite extraordinary.

LAWRENCE FOLLOWS **GABRIEL** TO THE BACK DOOR, AND THEY BOTH EXIT.

LONG PAUSE.

MARK: *Shit*, Stevie.

STEVIE: I want them out, Mark. I want to go to self-defence and I want them gone. I want to hear their car pull away and have them vanish.

MARK: You want to go to your class, so go to your class.

STEVIE: And leave *you* with *them*?

MARK: You don't want anything to do with it, so don't have anything to do with it. I'll get the information we need.

STEVIE: You don't even know the questions to ask. I don't think you even know you need to be asking questions.

MARK: So what if I probably did make the appointment because he's black? I read *The Guardian*, so shoot me.

STEVIE: I don't want to shoot you, Mark.

MARK: We agreed we'd get the information and then get them out.

STEVIE: I'd rather get them out now and cough up for a proper survey when I'm paid next .

MARK: A month? And if we don't have a month? If the wall –

STEVIE: We'll borrow it.

MARK: No! (Beat) I will take care of this. Go to your class.

STEVIE: I can't leave you with them, Marky. They know what they're doing.

MARK: I'll take care of it. I'll get the information we need –

STEVIE: We don't need information. We just need you to start functioning in the real world.

MARK: I'm trying to do that, Steve.

STEVIE: You don't walk out of jobs without discussing it first.

MARK: Christ – we've been through this.

STEVIE: You don't turn down decent work when we need the money.

MARK: We've been through this, Stevie. I do not typeset.

STEVIE: 'I do not typeset' – you stupid, selfish, *fucking* baby, I'm having our child here!

PAUSE.

SILENCE.

MARK: You don't think I can handle them, is that it?

STEVIE: Right now I don't trust you to handle your own cock without dropping or somehow breaking it.

MARK: Ta very much.

PAUSE.

STEVIE: I try so hard to respect your . . . what would you call it – your *integrity*, I suppose. I try and respect it. And I try and believe we're both investing in our *later*. But when you look at it face on, nothing you do is actually about *us*, Mark. It's all about you.

MARK: That's not true.

STEVIE: You can't even remember to bring my sweatshirt in out of the rain.

MARK: I genuinely forgot about the sweatshirt –

STEVIE: I'm not *talking* about the *sweatshirt*.

MARK: But you said 'you can't even' –

STEVIE EMITS A LOUD SCREAM OF FRUSTRATION. PAUSE.

STEVIE: When you walked out of the Post Office. Was it really spur of the moment? Or had you been planning it a while – keeping it secret 'til you actually did it?

MARK: Why would I do that?

STEVIE: Because you thought I'd've tried stopping you.

MARK: Would you have tried to stop me?

STEVIE: Was it spur of the moment?

PAUSE.

MARK: Yes.

STEVIE SIGHS WITH RELIEF, A WEIGHT LIFTING OFF HER. PAUSE. SHE CROSSES TO **MARK** AND TAKES HIS HEAD IN HER HANDS.

STEVIE: Marky, Marky, Marky . . . what are we going to do with you?

MARK: You can trust me, Stevie.

STEVIE: (She holds him tightly) I can trust you to go to down the road for a loaf of bread, Marky.

MARK: I'll do something.

STEVIE: What will you do?

MARK: Something to restore your trust in me.

STEVIE: What do you have in mind?

MARK: I don't know.

STEVIE: Think of something.

MARK: I'll . . . I'll . . . (Pause) What can I do?

STEVIE: I think you should think of something.

48

MARK: Okay. (Pause) What?

STEVIE: I can't tell you what to think.

MARK: I know.

STEVIE: Tell them to leave.

MARK: Tell them to leave?

STEVIE: Tell them to leave.

MARK: But we haven't got all the information.

STEVIE: We've got more than we want, which is more than enough. Tell them to go now.

MARK: And you'll trust me?

STEVIE: Tell them to leave now, Mark.

MARK: Does it matter I didn't think of it?

STEVIE: I just want them gone.

MARK: Okay.

STEVIE: Tell them to leave our house.

MARK: I will.

STEVIE: Now.

MARK: Then you can go to your class and I can get started on the nursery.

STEVIE: Tell them now.

PAUSE.

MARK: Biding my time, Stevie . . . holding back . . . choosing my moment. (Beat) It hasn't always been as easy as I imagined. For either of us. But it's going to pay off, Steve. Jesus . . . my book's gonna . . . it's gonna . . . believe me, Steven. It *really* is.

STEVIE: (Beat) I've been thinking about the book, Marky.

MARK: Okay.

STEVIE: (Beat) Surely 'R' is for bunny.

MARK: (Beat) Runny?

STEVIE: Rabbit.

MARK DISENTANGLES HIMSELF.

STEVIE: What I think I think about the book is that they should all be taxanomically correct, or all colloquial. One or the other, Marky. Not both.

MARK: That doesn't matter.

STEVIE: No, Marky. It *does* matter. You're not at college anymore. Things like this matter if you want to move forward.

MARK: But I've put so much into the bunny.

STEVIE: And it's beautiful. But wrong. It's not big, just . . . fundamental.

MARK: But 'B' has always been for bunny.

STEVIE: Then maybe 'M' should be for myxomatosis. Armadillo and bunny is patently inconsistent. It looks slip-shod. It smells amateur. You have to hit the ground running, Marky, or they'll leave you where you fall. You should've discussed your choices with me.

MARK: You've been waiting so long for this, I wanted to take your breath away.

STEVIE: We're up to our necks in each other, Mark. Don't you see? It's too late for amateur dramatics.

MARK: (Pointing to the back door) They said 'B' is for bunny is brilliant.

STEVIE: They'll tell you to put your shit on a stamp if it makes you warm to them. This is possibly your last chance, Marky. Make it work or . . .

MARK: Or what?

PAUSE.

STEVIE: Just make it work.

MARK: (Beat) Okay.

STEVIE: Good boy.

MARK: I'll tell them to leave now.

STEVIE: You do that.

MARK: I will.

STEVIE CROSSES TO THE KITCHEN DOOR.

STEVIE: I'll be in the front room. Come and find me when they've gone.

MARK: Moving forward now, Stevie.

STEVIE: (Nodding and smiling) Moving forward now, Marky.

STEVIE WATCHES AS **MARK** OPENS THE BACK DOOR AND GOES OUT. **STEVIE** STANDS ALONE FOR A MOMENT, THEN EXITS. THE KITCHEN IS EMPTY. AS **STEVIE** ENTERS THE FRONT ROOM THE LIGHTS DIM TO BLACK.

ACT TWO

(About 60 seconds later)

STEVIE SITS ALONE IN THE FRONT ROOM. THE DOOR IS CLOSED. THE KITCHEN IS EMPTY. THE BACK DOOR IS OPEN.

AFTER A MOMENT **MARK** ENTERS THROUGH THE BACK DOOR LOOKING A LITTLE NERVOUS. HE IS UNABLE TO SETTLE AND SHUFFLES ABOUT THE KITCHEN FOR A FEW SECONDS. **GABRIEL** THEN APPEARS AT THE BACK DOOR. HE HESITATES ON THE THRESHOLD AND REGARDS **MARK**.

LONG PAUSE.

GABRIEL: Nice little garden you've got out here.

MARK: (Beat) Yeah . . .

GABRIEL: Bit of work it'll be lovely.

MARK: (Beat) Uhuh.

GABRIEL: Fix the grass. Put up a swing. Beautiful for the little one when it comes.

MARK: Look, sorry . . . (Beat) I'm gonna have to ask you to leave.

GABRIEL: Should have a look at that slope though.

MARK: Thanks for coming all the same.

GABRIEL: You might find it lethal after a shower.

GABRIEL IMMEDIATELY KNOCKS TWICE ON THE BACK DOOR FRAME AND TAKES A STEP INTO THE KITCHEN.

LAWRENCE (Offstage. Loud) Gabriel, did I ever mention Cyril?

GABRIEL: Um, I don't believe you have, Mr D. Cyril who?

MARK: Did you hear me?

LAWRENCE: (Entering through the back door, talking) You'll also be interested in this, Mark, 'cause Cyril also works from home. Semi-detached in Forest Gate. He used to turn a lathe at Ford Dagenham, but now he produces hand-made cutlery for people without hands. Began as a one-off for his wife's cousin, horrifically dismembered in a boating accident. Some confusion whether or not a propeller on an outboard motor was actually rotating, so he reaches his hand into the water and finds, well, it was.

MARK: I'm afraid I'm going to have to ask you to –

LAWRENCE: So Cyril's wife asks Cyril to make this specialist item to give to the cousin for Christmas. Kid you not, it goes down an absolute bomb. The cousin loves it, the cousin's wife loves it – people with a perfectly good pair of hands want to place an order *just in case*. Within weeks Cyril's wife discovers there's an under-supplied market

51

for quality strap-on cutlery. Before he can blink she's set Cyril up in his own front room. He produces, she does the accounts. Word spreads. (Pausing for effect) Twenty years later she's still got him at it. This isn't my point. Now. (Pause) Every morning, without fail, Cyril gets up and dresses for business.

MARK: I'm sure this is going to be very interesting –

GABRIEL: 'Dresses for business', Mr D.?

LAWRENCE: Every morning for the past twenty years Cyril pops himself into a three piece suit and tie and goes downstairs to earn his living in his living room. Starts nine, come five-thirty, stops, goes upstairs, pops out of the formal-wear into something more casual.

GABRIEL: Chinos, Hawaiian beach shirt, moccasins?

LAWRENCE: I'm not privy to the ins and outs of his wardrobe. All I know is he doesn't leave the house the whole day.

MARK: You're going to have to go now.

LAWRENCE: For years I couldn't fathom this obsessive formality between nine and five-thirty. Then one hot evening over a cold lager I ask. 'Cy', I say. 'Cy, why the suit and tie when you work from home?'.

MARK: Come on, fellas. Did you hear what I said?

GABRIEL: What did he say?

LAWRENCE: So Cyril says, 'because I envy people who work in an office'. What does this mean? So I say, 'Cy, what do you mean?'. And Cyril says, 'because they have a place to be during daylight'. (Pause) This is my point: *a place to be.*

MARK: You *have* to leave.

LAWRENCE: See my point, Mark?

MARK: You have to leave *now.*

LAWRENCE: No, my point is that Cyril was a deeply confused individual. Still is, despite branching out to meet an expanding market for essential utensils for the contemporary amputee. But, I suppose that's what happens if you let your destiny be dictated to by another.

GABRIEL: To completely lose sight of yourself like that must be appalling, Mr D. To lose twenty years to the dictat of your *spouse* must be unthinkable.

LAWRENCE: It doesn't bear thinking about.

GABRIEL: To be under the thumb of your partner to that extent . . . I'd sooner put a bullet through the roof of my mouth.

LAWRENCE: What do you think, Mark?

MARK: I'm afraid you have to go.

LAWRENCE: Both of us?

MARK: Yes.

LAWRENCE: Really?

MARK: Yeah.

LAWRENCE: I see.

PAUSE.

GABRIEL: Is that what Stevie told you to tell us?

PAUSE. **MARK** CROSSES TO THE KITCHEN DOOR AND HOLDS IT OPEN.

MARK: Thanks very much for the estimate.

MARK OPENS THE DOOR WIDER.

LAWRENCE: Don't thank us for something we haven't yet done. You surely can't expect us to abandon you with your house in such a state?

MARK: Look . . . I appreciate your concern. (Opening the door wider) Please . . .

PAUSE.

LAWRENCE: (Approaching slowly) Mark, you mustn't feel embarrassed. This happens all the time. From our viewpoint it's actually quite endearing.

MARK: I'm not embarrassed.

GABRIEL: Why don't you come and sit down?

MARK: I don't want to sit down.

LAWRENCE: Tell a man something's wrong with his property he wants to storm out and fix it on the spot. Tell a woman and they stick their head in the sand and, let's face this right now, they make a loud, stupid noise.

GABRIEL: Come and sit down, Mark. You look tired. I expect you've been working too hard on your wonderful pictures.

MARK: I don't want to sit down. I just want you to –

GABRIEL: Women share their lives with men so they live in a constant state of denial. Fortunately that's their problem not ours, but it can be potentially disruptive. Such as now. We see this all the time: dismiss the doctor for his diagnosis. She wants us out. She's panicking. I'm afraid it's nothing more exotic than good old fashioned panic.

LAWRENCE: We're speaking as one man to another here, Mark.

GABRIEL: Though in our current situation, two men.

MARK: You've got to leave.

LAWRENCE: We have a responsibility to fulfil.

MARK: You've got to go.

LAWRENCE: You don't mean that. I know you don't. Because this is coming from *her*.

MARK: I've got to make you leave.

LAWRENCE: Why?

MARK: 'Scuse me but I don't have to explain myself.

LAWRENCE: After all we've done for you, you don't think you owe us an explanation for casting us out without a fair hearing?

GABRIEL: Why don't you sit down, Mark?

MARK: I don't want to sit down. If I make you leave her trust –

LAWRENCE: Her *trust*?

MARK: Stevie's trust in me . . . look . . . you don't have to understand.

GABRIEL: I think we understand more than you think.

PAUSE.

MARK: If I make you go Stevie's trust will be restored. So you have to go.

PAUSE.

LAWRENCE: Her trust will be restored if you make us go? What is this, relationship kindergarten? You do this, that proves that? Is this how you live today? You bought a house together, you're making a baby together, and you've only got as far as *obedience school*?

MARK: Look –

LAWRENCE: No Mark, *you* look. And listen. *Trust* isn't some ball you bounce around and confiscate when and where you get the urge. Trust is the permanent bedrock. It's the belief between two people binding them together when the bottom drops off their world. My God, when a man loses his business at the age of

fifty two –

GABRIEL: Mr Davidson.

LAWRENCE: (Raising a hand to halt **GABRIEL**, and moving closer to **MARK**) (Pause) When a man loses his business, Mark, at the age of fifty two. And he returns home reeking of the scrap-heap. When he no longer has anything in his pockets but pocket. And even the confidence to choose a morning paper from the newsagent's rack has drained from his fingers. When he cries like a baby at the drop of a hat. And yet his wife of thirty-one years – his *partner* – will still stand by his side holding an umbrella in a blizzard. *That* . . . now *that* my friend, is *trust*.

PAUSE.

GABRIEL: Let's be sensible about this, Mark. Let's be civilised. Why don't we all just sit down and calm down.

GABRIEL SITS AT THE TABLE. **LAWRENCE** SITS AT THE TABLE. **GABRIEL** PULLS OUT A CHAIR FOR **MARK**.

GABRIEL: Mark?

MARK: You really do have to go.

GABRIEL: Of course. In good time.

LAWRENCE: Sit with us, Mark. Sit down and discuss this calmly. Like men.

PAUSE.

MARK: Only for a minute.

GABRIEL: Take as long as you need.

MARK JOINS THE MEN AT THE TABLE. PAUSE.

GABRIEL: So you fixed this appointment because I'm black.

MARK: I'm *really* sorry she said that.

GABRIEL: So it's true?

MARK: Look . . . When I was at college I marched . . . signed petitions . . . If you know me you'd know I'm the last person in the world you'd accuse of anything like that.

GABRIEL: You just feel sorry for black boys in sharp suits deluding themselves they're on a par with Whitey, is that it?

MARK: I don't need this right now.

GABRIEL: Try putting yourself in my shoes on a daily basis.

MARK: Is it so terrible to –

GABRIEL: To what? Take pity on a wog?

MARK: I really do *not* need this right now. I thought I was doing you a favour.

GABRIEL: Doing me a favour? I've heard it called many things but 'doing me favour'. Why don't you do us both a favour, *brother*, and stop trying to justify your prejudice.

MARK: No – I know what it's like going from one door to the next hawking your stuff round. I understand –

GABRIEL: What did you say? *Hawking*? Excuse me, I do not *hawk*. I am not in the *hawking* business. You may be in the *hawking* business but I'm not. I am a *pro-fessional*. I am not some NIGGER you can –

MARK: All right, whatever. (Beat) Whatever you say. I'm sorry. I'm really sorry you took it that way. I didn't mean you to take it that way but if you took it that way, I'm really sorry.

GABRIEL: Now don't whitewash me, Mark.

LAWRENCE: (Cutting in) *Gabriel*.

GABRIEL: What?

LAWRENCE: What . . . *who*?

GABRIEL: (Pause) What, 'Mr Davidson'.

LAWRENCE: Better. Now button it.

GABRIEL: Sorry.

LAWRENCE: We're here for Mark and Stevie's benefit, not to let your persecution complex off it's lead.

PAUSE. **LAWRENCE** STEADIES **GABRIEL** WITH HIS EYES.

GABRIEL: I'm sorry.

LAWRENCE: Don't apologise to *me*.

GABRIEL: (Beat) I'm sorry, Mark.

LAWRENCE: You want to be a professional then *be* a professional.

GABRIEL: I'm –

LAWRENCE: Just *schtum* it.

MARK: There's no need to . . . you really shouldn't treat him like this in front of –

LAWRENCE: (Sharply) Please allow me the liberty of treating my staff as I see fit, Mark.

MARK: Jesus. I don't need any of this. I give you an appointment to help you out – turns out I'm some kind of *bigot*. She says I'm selfish, weak . . . tells me to throw you out . . . throw out 'B' is for bunny. I do all this stuff for *everyone* else and I'm *still* the fucking bad guy.

GABRIEL: Stevie told you to dump 'B' is for bunny?

MARK: (Beat) She says it's *inconsistent*.

GABRIEL: But it's superb.

MARK: She says it's too *colloquial*.

GABRIEL: Does colloquial matter?

MARK: *I* didn't think so.

GABRIEL: My kid –

LAWRENCE: Kids.

GABRIEL: My kids, I *know*, would love 'B' is for bunny. You can't be too cut and dried. There's no such thing as a rule when it comes to children. They're a law unto themselves.

LAWRENCE: That picture's a beautiful piece of work, Mark. No question about that.

MARK: I've been working on the bunny alone for a month solid. Which is on top of the six weeks on the armadillo and the *years* it's taken me to acquire and perfect the technique. You make one false mark and all you have at the end of your fingers is firewood. You can't bluff this. You can't cut and paste this. It's 100% excellence 100% of the time. Any day now they'll bring out some software to match what I do with my hands. But not yet. Jesus . . . I haven't seen my bed in four days, and that's the honest truth.

GABRIEL: Didn't I say he looked tired, Mr D?

LAWRENCE: You did.

GABRIEL: Listen to me, Mark. Anyone in touch with the child within would fall for your book on 'B' is for bunny alone. I'm only talking from a gut reaction –

MARK: Gut reaction – it's the gut reaction I want. Kids don't theorise, they like or they don't like.

56

GABRIEL: In my opinion . . . and it's just my opinion . . . you'd be crazy to chuck out the bunny. Don't you think so, Mr D.?

LAWRENCE: Can you see Michelangelo going at the Sistine Chapel with a rubber because he overheard some priest carping in a cloister?

GABRIEL: You really should have more faith in your own judgement.

MARK: God knows I try.

GABRIEL: You're a supremely gifted individual, Mark. Any fool can see that.

MARK: Who cares? Today it's crap floating on the surface not cream.

LAWRENCE: I've got a theory about 'today', and my theory about 'today' is that most people would rather live circa 1958. I know I would.

GABRIEL: Crap will always float, Mark, 'cause people are scared of the future, mystified by the present and generally ignorant of the past. We need a distraction from total bewilderment and crap provides that.

MARK: I can't do crap.

GABRIEL: That's why you're so special. You couldn't produce crap if you tried.

MARK: I have tried.

GABRIEL: And?

MARK: I couldn't do it.

GABRIEL: And why not?

MARK: Because I'm crap at crap.

GABRIEL: Because you have the rarest of gifts: that of being *yourself*. (Beat) You're your own man, Mark. How many people today can honestly say that about themselves? I know I can't. I know Mr Davidson can't.

MARK: I've always *tried* to be true to myself.

GABRIEL: Don't let anyone take it from you.

MARK: I try not to.

GABRIEL: And by anyone I mean *anyone*. Whoever he, or *she*, might be.

PAUSE.

MARK: Look . . . before . . . I'm sorry if you thought I was –

GABRIEL: Forget it, man. It's easier to jump to a fashionable conclusion than take the trouble to think past the knee-jerk response.

MARK: Try telling that to Stevie.

GABRIEL: Between you and me women have a lot of things on their mind. And none of them is logic.

GABRIEL STANDS, PATS **LAWRENCE** ON THE SHOULDER, AND MOVES AWAY.

LAWRENCE: I'm going to ask you a simple question, Mark. And I want you to answer in complete honesty. If you are knowingly dishonest in your answer the consequences scarcely bear thinking about.

MARK: What question?

LAWRENCE: My question is this: if money was no object, would you not have Ex-Cote applied to this house without hesitation?

PAUSE.

LAWRENCE: Without hesitation, Mark.

MARK: Well . . .

LAWRENCE: You're hesitating, which is something I distinctly advised you against. Sometimes you've got to by-pass the conscious mind to gain access to the truth.

MARK: If money was no object?

LAWRENCE: Forget money. In a world without money, Mark, Would you or would you not?

MARK: I suppose . . .

LAWRENCE: You *suppose*?

MARK: In a world without money wouldn't everyone?

LAWRENCE: Evidence suggests otherwise.

MARK: Okay. In a world without money I'd have to say I would.

LAWRENCE: *And yet.*

MARK: And yet what?

LAWRENCE: And yet the world is not without money.

MARK: That's true.

LAWRENCE: In fact, we're regularly informed money makes the world go round. As well as being the oil on the wheel, money is increasingly the wheel itself.

MARK: I know.

LAWRENCE: *And yet.*

MARK: And yet?

LAWRENCE: And yet what if I was to tell you . . . as far as Ex-Cote is concerned . . . money needn't be a worry?

MARK: I'd have to say I'd be interested in what you had to say on that topic.

LAWRENCE: And Stevie?

MARK: Um, I don't think Stevie'd be interested in what you had to say on any topic.

LAWRENCE: She's sitting in, in, where's she sitting exactly?

MARK: The front room. Waiting for me to tell her you've gone.

LAWRENCE: So there she sits, telling herself the walls are fine. But we three know otherwise. Someone has to face reality, Mark. Someone has to take responsibility for the long-term well-being of your family.

MARK: She thinks I don't live in the real world.

LAWRENCE: In a world of quicksand we have to know where we stand, and stand there.

MARK: But money –

GABRIEL: You want to talk about money?

MARK: It's a big obstacle.

LAWRENCE: I have a theory about big obstacles. And my theory about big obstacles is they can generally be got round.

MARK: But Stevie –

LAWRENCE: What did I just say about obstacles?

GABRIEL: The family home's in trouble, Mark. You know that, don't you?

MARK: I . . . it seems so.

LAWRENCE: Not seems. *Is.* Ex-Cote can save this lovely house, Mark. It can rectify the damage and safeguard it against the future.

MARK: If you say so.

LAWRENCE: You want a second opinion? Quite right. Gabriel?

GABRIEL: Without question.

LAWRENCE: Stevie told you to ask us to leave, and we could do that, and that'd be the quick way out of this situation. For now.

GABRIEL: But tomorrow?

MARK: That's what I said. I as good as said those exact words.

LAWRENCE: You're now behoven not to panic, but to keep a level head and summon up a little steel. A foot has got to be put down before things get out of hand. And I'm sorry, but I have to say this. This may sound old fashioned to your ears, but if my wife felt she couldn't trust *me* I would frankly feel *grossly* insulted.

MARK: I did feel insulted.

LAWRENCE: As would any man. And feel free to quote me on that.

MARK: This is my house too. Just 'cause I don't *physically* contribute 'money' to the mortgage. *Yet.*

LAWRENCE: Then let's save and protect your house, Mark. At Ex-Cote we say money should never be allowed to get in the way of common sense. It's a free estimate, Mark. And I give you my personal guarantee it costs less than you think.

MARK: I don't have anything to apologise for.

LAWRENCE: I like a man who knows his own mind. I used to like Cyril. But now . . . tell me what's left to like?

MARK: (To **GABRIEL**) Do *you* think I've got anything to apologise for?

GABRIEL: Probably. (Smiling) But that's no reason why you should.

MARK: We should at least hear the cost before rejecting it outright.

LAWRENCE: It's the only responsible course of action. Make a stand.

MARK: (Standing) I'm going to.

LAWRENCE: Good for you!

MARK: Can I go to the toilet first?

LAWRENCE: Be our guest.

MARK: It's all this tea. I'll have a quick slash, then I'll get Stevie in here.

MARK EXITS THE KITCHEN. **LAWRENCE** SLOWLY SINKS ONTO THE TABLE WITH A SIGH OF EXHAUSTION. **GABRIEL** TAKES A PACK OF CIGARETTES FROM HIS JACKET AND LIGHTS ONE. HE TAKES A LONG DRAG. EXHALES. PAUSE.

LAWRENCE: I don't think I can do this.

GABRIEL: Don't bleat, Larry, you're doing it.

LAWRENCE: I really don't think I'm cut out for this.

GABRIEL: This is the way it is, and it's painful but necessary. The punter used to at least have some idea what he wanted, he just needed persuasion to part with his money to pay for it. Now they have to be persuaded as to what they want as well. Everyone thinks they're now above this. Everyone thinks they're now smarter than this. Which they are. Except that this isn't what this is about. Be direct. You only have to look at the fast-food industry to see it works. Twenty years ago Big Mac was a centre-forward for Newcastle. Now it's brunch, lunch and supper for the munch bunch across the entire planet. It's a world of competing interests, and it's our responsibility to compete better. It's not a confidence trick, simply . . . *confidence.*

LAWRENCE: Feels like I'm banging my head against a brick wall.

GABRIEL: Not a wall, Lawrence, a stone. And inside every stone there's a single drop of blood, which is what we're after. We have to squeeze, and keep squeezing. Giving blood is a good thing. It's vital. But they still won't do it without persuasion.

PAUSE.

LAWRENCE: Did you have to say *nigger*?

GABRIEL: His bleating was getting on my nerves. I don't give a monkey's toss why I'm in the house as long as I'm in the house. But don't bleat at me.

LAWRENCE: Did I slap you down too hard?

GABRIEL: As long as it brings the desired effect there's no such thing as *too* anything. You pulled him closer to your position and earned his respect. Just bear in mind there's no such thing as the perfect couple.

60

Feel for the cracks and apply pressure. Divide and conquer. First one. Then both. It's the science of Stress. (Takes out a packet of Marlboro) I'll be outside inhaling my lunch.

GABRIEL CROSSES TO THE BACK DOOR.

LAWRENCE: Could I have a glass of water?

GABRIEL: (Exiting) Of course. Help yourself.

LAWRENCE: No. I meant –

GABRIEL HAS GONE OUT OF THE BACK DOOR. PAUSE. **LAWRENCE** MAKES TO GET UP FROM HIS CHAIR BUT CAN'T FIND THE ENERGY AND SLUMPS BACK DOWN. HE SIGHS WITH AN ANCIENT FATIGUE.

LAWRENCE: (To **GABRIEL** offstage) When the business went under my wife said I should grease my old contacts. Follow up thirty years of connections. (Pause) I meant to write a few letters. But time slipped away. (Pause) (Quieter. To self) I shouldn't be here. I'm a poultry man. I should be up to my wrist in a chicken.

LONG PAUSE.

STEVIE HAS BEEN SLOWLY PACING THE **FRONT ROOM** FOR SEVERAL MINUTES. AFTER A FEW MOMENTS **MARK** ENTERS. **STEVIE** REGARDS HIM FOR A MOMENT.

STEVIE: Have they gone?

MARK: I told them to go.

STEVIE: You told them?

MARK: In no uncertain terms.

STEVIE: You were firm with them?

MARK: I was.

STEVIE SIGHS WITH RELIEF, PUTS HER ARMS ROUND **MARK**, AND KISSES HIM.

STEVIE: Thank you.

MARK: Stevie –

STEVIE: Before. It was sheer frustration more than anything.

MARK: Stevie –

STEVIE: Since we moved everything's felt so fragile. I know I've been a complete bitch, Marky. I just want everything to come right in time for the baby. Everything in place. The house. You. *Us.*

MARK: Stevie –

STEVIE: No, let me get this out. It's been on my mind, and I've known couples split up over less.

MARK: Stevie –

STEVIE: Deb dumped Al simply because he couldn't go down on her.

MARK: What?

STEVIE: True. Whenever he stuck his face in her groin he started sneezing. What with the absence of satisfaction, noise, and nasal discharge I guess it wore her down.

MARK: She dumped him for *sneezing*?

STEVIE: All over her fanny, Mark. Context is all important.

MARK: So what's this thing on your mind?

STEVIE: It's nothing . . . specific.

MARK: A non-specific something?

STEVIE: More a general feeling of . . .

MARK: Of what?

STEVIE: Perhaps it's hormonal. I'm starting to be riddled with hormones now. It's just recently . . . I've become aware of this creeping feeling of . . . I don't know . . . *stagnation* I suppose.

MARK: You feel we're stagnating?

STEVIE: We've been – (Beat) Perhaps there's a better way of putting it. Sometimes, recently, when I've come home from work. I look at you and . . . I don't know.

MARK: You don't know what? Who I am? Where you are?

STEVIE: I come home form work to see you kneeling on the carpet in your underpants, sketching animals, and I want to put my fist through a door.

PAUSE.

MARK: Which door?

STEVIE: Any door. The front door.

MARK: The front door?

STEVIE: Yeah.

MARK: That's a thick door, Stevie.

STEVIE: I know.

PAUSE.

MARK: I see.

STEVIE: I'm not having a dig.

MARK: I see.

STEVIE: I said some stuff earlier. Maybe we both said some stuff that needed saying. We cleared some air and that has to be better in the long term. I was beginning to think that maybe we'd terminally lost the plot. But when you said 'moving forward now, Stevie' my heart leapt.

MARK: Sorry.

STEVIE: No – with joy!

MARK: Stevie –

STEVIE: No. I've said all I've got to say, and that is all there is to say.

62

STEVIE GENTLY KISSES **MARK**. SHE HUGS HIM TIGHTLY.

STEVIE: I love you, Marky.

HAVING FINISHED HIS CIGARETTE, **GABRIEL** NOW
RETURNS INTO THE KITCHEN AND LOOKS AT HIS WATCH.

GABRIEL: Tick tock tick tock.

LAWRENCE: Shouldn't we wait? Don't want to panic them.

GABRIEL: Every time he disappears like this it's like starting from
scratch. Go and get them back. To achieve closure we must close. Get
them back and let's finish this before we forget why we're here.

MARK: About this afternoon, Stevie.

STEVIE: Hugging now. Hugging and moving forward now.

GABRIEL RE-ARRANGES THE CHAIRS. **LAWRENCE** STANDS.

MARK: About the salesmen. About the salesmen . . . *leaving.*

LAWRENCE SLOWLY EXITS THE KITCHEN.

STEVIE: Sssh . . . (Her eyes now closed. Smiling) Can you feel it?
(Pressing her stomach close against him) Can you feel our baby
growing?

LAWRENCE OPENS THE DOOR. PAUSE.

LAWRENCE: Now that's what I like to see. Young lovers. Loving
each other.

STEVIE IMMEDIATELY PUSHES **MARK** AWAY IN AN
IMPULSE OF SURPRISE.

MARK: Stephen . . .

STEVIE: How did you get back in?

LAWRENCE: Sorry?

STEVIE: Have you forgotten something?

MARK: Stevie . . .

LAWRENCE: I'm still here because I haven't gone.

STEVIE: No, no, no, no, Mark said – you said they've gone.

MARK: Stevie, I said I *told* them to go.

STEVIE: You said –

LAWRENCE: You want to know how much Ex-Cote costs? So come
and find out. My experience of Ex-Cote is you think you don't need it
but you do. You think you won't want it but you will. You think you
can't afford it but you can. Tea?

MARK: No more tea.

LAWRENCE: It's your house.

LAWRENCE EXITS, LEAVING THE DOOR OPEN. HE RETURNS
TO THE KITCHEN. PAUSE.

STEVIE: Why didn't you tell them to go? You said you were going to tell them to go.

MARK: Stevie, *trust* me.

STEVIE: You said you were going to *do something*. (More insistent) You said you were going to tell them to go!

MARK: Our house is falling down, Steve. I can't let that happen. There's no need to panic.

STEVIE: I'm not panicking!

MARK: They've seen this a hundred times.

STEVIE: Seen what a hundred times?

MARK: This. You. You like this.

STEVIE: (Suddenly very alarmed) Mark, tell me you haven't signed anything.

MARK: I haven't signed a thing. Don't worry.

STEVIE: How am I not supposed to worry?

MARK: It's simple.

STEVIE: What is?

MARK: Just *trust* me. All you have to do now is *trust* me.

MARK KISSES STEVIE.

GABRIEL: Just remember: we are telling, not selling.

MARK EXITS AND CROSSES INTO THE KITCHEN, WHERE HE SITS AT THE TABLE.

STEVIE: What about my class? (Exiting after **MARK**) Mark? Mark!

GABRIEL: What was it you said, Mr Davidson? About a 'loud stupid noise'?

THE MEN LAUGH. STEVIE ENTERS TO THE DISSIPATING SOUND OF THEIR DERISION. SHE STOPS A YARD OR TWO BEYOND THE THRESHOLD. PAUSE.

LAWRENCE: Stevie, is it truly wise for a woman in your condition to be rushing around in a class?

MARK: I said that.

GABRIEL: Any responsible father-to-be would say the same to his pregnant partner.

STEVIE: Mark, what are you doing?

LAWRENCE: Mark's accepting responsibility for the situation, Stevie.

GABRIEL: Mark has agreed that if money were no object he'd have Ex-Cote without hesitation.

LAWRENCE: So we're about to show you both how to enjoy the full protection of Ex-Cote.

MARK: I can't gamble the future of my family on a gesture, Stevie. I can't and I won't. The situation behoves me to be bigger than that.

STEVIE: The situation *behoves* you?

MARK: I am behoved. Someone's got to be objective. Side-step emotional outburst and keep a level head. But I can't do it by myself, Stevie. I need your trust on this.

STEVIE: Marky, I thought we settled this. *In the other room.*

MARK: Yes we did.

STEVIE: You wanted me to trust you in the other room. You asked me how. And I told you.

MARK: No.

STEVIE: No?

MARK: I'm talking about *trust*, not *obedience*. Let's be mature about this, Stevie. Let's act our age now.

STEVIE: Obedience. What do you mean *obedience*?

MARK: Because if you can't trust me, Stevie, well, what's the point?

STEVIE: What's the point?

LAWRENCE: Mark's got a point, Stevie. Without trust it's like riding a tandem with just one of you peddling.

GABRIEL: Leading to cramp, muscular spasm, exhaustion. And then you drop off the bike.

LAWRENCE: Or the bike crashes. Or you anticipate the crash and alight without serious injury.

GABRIEL: Taking a bus home. One upstairs, one down.

LAWRENCE: Or a train.

GABRIEL: Separate carriages?

LAWRENCE: Oh, I'd think so by then, wouldn't you?

MARK: I listened to what they had to say about the house, Stevie. And now I need you to trust me to make the right decision.

STEVIE: The right decision was to ask them to leave. The *right* decision was not to have asked them back in the first place.

MARK: I want you to trust me enough to stand next to me in a blizzard.

STEVIE: To stand – to where?

MARK: With an umbrella. Because trust isn't some ball you bounce, Steve.

STEVIE: Mark, I don't know what you're talking about.

MARK: It's deeper than a ball. Don't you see?

STEVIE: What is?

MARK: It's the bottom bedrock.

PAUSE.

STEVIE: Okay. You've had your fun. Now go.

LAWRENCE: *Fun?*

STEVIE: You've turned my boyfriend into a gibbering fool – so, well done, but now go.

GABRIEL: We have a duty to stay. When I look at Mark, Stevie, I don't see a gibbering fool. I see a man uniquely himself, prepared to do right by his family. And I take my hat off to him.

MARK: They see this all the time, Stephen. It's nothing more exotic than plain old-fashioned panic.

STEVIE: Get out.

MARK: I want them to stay, Stevie. I think they should stay. They may be in a position to help us.

STEVIE: Marky?

MARK: We need them to stay.

STEVIE LOOKS BETWEEN THE THREE MEN FACING HER. PAUSE.

STEVIE: Okay. (Pause) (She smiles) All right. Give me the contract.

LAWRENCE: What contract?

STEVIE: You've brought something for us to sign. So I want to give my signature. I want the contract, and I want to sign it.

LAWRENCE: I'm sorry, Stevie, but all I've got at the moment is a pencil and a piece of paper.

STEVIE: I want the, whatever you call it. I want to sign it. The contract? The form? The agreement? Whatever you've got, I'll sign it for you now.

SHE SITS AT THE TABLE.

STEVIE: So give me the papers.

LAWRENCE MAKES A MOVE TO THE BRIEFCASE THAT HAS BEEN BROUGHT IN, BUT IS STOPPED BY **GABRIEL**. PAUSE.

GABRIEL: And then what?

STEVIE: And then I sign the papers.

GABRIEL: And then what?

STEVIE: And then Mark signs the papers.

GABRIEL: And then what?

STEVIE: And then you leave.

GABRIEL: And then what?

STEVIE: And then we have Ex-Cote, and the world spins faster for a moment out of sheer delight.

PAUSE.

66

GABRIEL: No.

STEVIE: No?

GABRIEL: I don't think so.

STEVIE: You don't?

GABRIEL: No. I don't think so. I think once we've gone you call the office and cancel.

PAUSE.

STEVIE: I wouldn't do that.

GABRIEL: We've seen it a thousand times. And there really is no point speaking with that in mind.

STEVIE: I would not do that. Trust me.

GABRIEL: (Smiling) It's perfectly natural.

STEVIE: *Trust* me.

GABRIEL: It's exactly what you would do. Wouldn't she, Mark?

PAUSE.

GABRIEL: Mark?

PAUSE.

MARK: You know you would, Stevie.

STEVIE: I don't believe you just said that . . .

LAWRENCE: It's perfectly natural.

GABRIEL: In a world that's merely one prop in a cola commercial it's wise to be sceptical. Who is who they seem? Which of us can, with one hundred per cent confidence, still call a spade a spade?

LAWRENCE: The only people you can truly trust are mum and dad. Even then, dad probably has a closet bristling with skeletons.

STEVIE: My father died of cancer when I was six.

PAUSE.

LAWRENCE: Her father died of cancer when she was six.

GABRIEL: I'm so sorry.

MARK: He smoked 60 a day.

LAWRENCE: Disgusting habit. And potentially lethal.

GABRIEL: Strength of character is frequently distilled from a tragic circumstance. Listen, Stevie. In the old days if someone wanted your money they hit you over the head and did a runner with your purse. Today mugging *is* a mugs' game. Certainly, you could sign up for Ex-Cote and then cancel the second we leave the premises. But better yet. Why not make an informed choice? For a split second suspend your belief that I'm a shark and he's an arsehole –

STEVIE: Actually, I had it round the other way.

GABRIEL: (Smiling) The customer is always right. But why not, for a moment, lay yourself open to the truth?

MARK: She used to have an open mind. In college –

GABRIEL: Yes, Mark. I'm sure. Mr D. The truth?

LAWRENCE TAKES THE POLAROIDS FROM HIS POCKET AND PUTS THEM ON THE TABLE BEFORE **STEVIE**.

LAWRENCE: The Truth, Stevie. In all the colours of the rainbow. Whatever else, a picture is still worth a thousand words.

STEVIE: You know I've missed my class.

GABRIEL: So what have you now got to lose by listening?

MARK: Nothing! Don't you see, Steve?!

GABRIEL: I was talking to Stevie.

MARK: Sorry.

LAWRENCE: I've got a theory about missing your class. And my theory about missing your class is that, in the long term, you'll be happy you missed it.

STEVIE: Look . . . this is a waste of time. We simply don't have the money.

MARK: Money's no object, Stevie.

LAWRENCE: This isn't about fitting a Jacuzzi. Or a conservatory. Or some ornamental footspa. We are not talking about a lxury item. It's not about what you want, but what you *need*. And money must always be no object for what you need, Stevie. (Unseen by **STEVIE** or **MARK** he motions to **GABRIEL** to close the kitchen door) That's what we're here to help you understand.

GABRIEL QUIETLY CROSSES TO THE DOOR AND CLOSES IT.

STEVIE: But what you don't understand is we only have my income.

MARK: At the moment.

STEVIE: At the moment.

MARK: When my book –

STEVIE: (Cutting in) We just about get by.

GABRIEL NODS AT **LAWRENCE**. **LAWRENCE** TAKES OUT A PIECE OF PAPER AND A PENCIL FROM HIS JACKET.

LAWRENCE: I'm now holding a piece of paper and a pencil. Bear with me now. I want you to jot down how much you think a builder would charge to paint the exterior of your house. (Laying the paper and pencil on the table) Front and back.

STEVIE: I've got no idea.

LAWRENCE: I know you don't. Estimate.

STEVIE: I have no basis upon which to estimate.

LAWRENCE: Make an educated guess.

STEVIE: I don't know anything about paint.

LAWRENCE: An uneducated guess then.

STEVIE: I don't guess. I hate guessing.

MARK: Steven really hates guessing.

LAWRENCE: Just take a shot in the dark.

MARK: Fifteen hundred pounds.

PAUSE.

LAWRENCE: Fifteen hundred? That's the figure you want to jot down, is it?

MARK: That's my estimate.

LAWRENCE: Then jot that down.

MARK: I just told you. Do I have to jot it down?

LAWRENCE: That's why we bring pencil and paper. It helps to keep a record.

MARK TAKES THE PENCIL AND PAPER AND WRITES DOWN THE FIGURE.

STEVIE: This is a complete waste of time.

LAWRENCE: Now fold the paper.

MARK FOLDS THE PAPER.

LAWRENCE: Now give me the paper.

MARK GIVES THE PAPER TO **LAWRENCE**. **LAWRENCE** OPENS THE PAPER. PAUSE.

LAWRENCE: Are you serious? Fifteen hundred? C'mon. Be serious.

MARK: That's my guess. That's my estimate.

LAWRENCE: Fifteen hundred? (Showing the paper to **GABRIEL**) Is he serious?

GABRIEL: I *estimate* he is, Mr D.

LAWRENCE: No, Mark. Be serious.

MARK: I'm being serious.

LAWRENCE: Fifteen hundred? *C'mon*. I'm being serious, Mark. You be serious too.

MARK: All right. Fifteen *thousand*!

PAUSE. **LAWRENCE** LOOKS AT **MARK** BLANKLY.

LAWRENCE: To save argument I'll tell you how much a builder would charge. (Pause) Five and a half thousand pounds.

MARK: For a paint job?

STEVIE: Front and back?

LAWRENCE: Front and back. I won't bore you with the details.

MARK: Five and a half thousand pounds?

LAWRENCE: And that's being conservative. Now. At Ex-Cote we guarantee our product for – guess how long?

STEVIE: I told you I hate –

LAWRENCE: Have a stab. Go on. Stab away.

STEVIE: Eternity.

LAWRENCE: No. (Pause) Not eternity. Twenty-five years.

STEVIE: That was going to be my next guess. Eternity . . . then twenty-five years.

LAWRENCE: In twenty-five years guess how many times you'd have to have that builder back to re-paint the house?

STEVIE: Jesus, how many times do I have to – okay. As many times as we want.

LAWRENCE: I'm not talking about how many you'd *want* to have your property re-painted. I'm talking about how many times you'd *need* to.

MARK: How many we'd need to?

STEVIE: I give up.

LAWRENCE: Mark?

MARK: Well –

STEVIE: He gives up as well.

PAUSE.

LAWRENCE: Okay. Your house would need a conventional re-paint approximately . . . Gabriel?

GABRIEL: Approximately every five years.

LAWRENCE: Which at £5,500 a time, five times within a twenty-five year period, would cost you the best part of –

STEVIE: Twenty-seven and a half thousand pounds.

LAWRENCE: The best part of thirty thousand pounds.

STEVIE: Twenty-seven and a half thousand pounds.

LAWRENCE: Like I said, the best part of thirty thousand pounds. *Thirty-thousand pounds.* I'm jotting that down. Think about it while I jot. (Writing on the paper) Thirty thousand pounds. In other words: a great deal of money. Now I'm going to jot down another number on this piece of paper. After I've jotted it we're going to leave it with you to consider in private. Because at Ex-Cote we don't believe in pressure. We don't have to, because we believe the product speaks for itself.

LAWRENCE WRITES ON THE PAPER, THEN FOLDS IT OVER.

LAWRENCE: I've now written on the paper, and I'm now leaving the paper on the table. Stevie. Before. You wanted to know 'how much'. (He taps the paper) So here's how *little*.

LAWRENCE EXITS THE KITCHEN AND ENTERS THE FRONT ROOM, WHERE HE TAKES OUT A HANDKERCHIEF AND MOPS HIS BROW. HE LEANS AGAINST THE MANTELPIECE FOR SUPPORT. **GABRIEL** FOLLOWS BEHIND, STOPPING AT THE KITCHEN DOOR.

GABRIEL: Take your time. Think it through, and make the right decision for you . . . and for your family to come.

GABRIEL EXITS INTO THE FRONT ROOM. IN THE KITCHEN **MARK** REGARDS THE FOLDED PAPER. **STEVIE** CANNOT LOOK AT EITHER THE PAPER OR **MARK**.

PAUSE.

STEVIE: You were going to start the nursery this afternoon. 'I'll start Saturday' you said.

MARK: And if the walls fall down all we'll have is nursery-coloured rubble.

PAUSE.

LAWRENCE: I'm too old for this . . .

GABRIEL: When you close you'll feel the years melt away. I've seen it happen. Men of forty emerge through sixty year old wrinkles. I promise you, Lawrence there is *nothing* on this Earth like a close.

LAWRENCE: She could be my own daughter, Mr James. For all I know someone like me might be round there right now, doing this to them.

GABRIEL: Mark and Stevie could do a lot worse than Ex-Cote, Larry. A lot worse. I should know. I sold a lot worse for years.

STEVIE: You walk into a room and catch a glimpse of something you've never seen before. You tell yourself you want it. You convince yourself you can't live without it . . .

MARK: (Looking round the kitchen) Don't blame yourself, Steve. Everyone's a sucker for a re-possession with original features and a south-facing garden. How could we know?

LAWRENCE: I don't think my daughter could withstand this, Mr James.

GABRIEL: Help is often difficult to accept when first offered. But make no mistake: they need our help, Lawrence. They're lost in the woods. But we can lead them to a place of safety.

STEVIE: I didn't walk into this blind. I knew we had to work to make it work.

MARK: Goes without saying. Wallpaper. Paint. Stripping down the stair-rails.

LAWRENCE: But they don't need Ex-Cote, Mr James.

GABRIEL: They don't know what they need. Remember your training.

LAWRENCE: God knows I know the theory . . .

STEVIE: But *this*. I didn't account for this, Mark.

MARK: We didn't know, Stevie. How could we have known?

LAWRENCE: A kid on the way. Him jobless, pinning the future on an anteater and a bunny. Doesn't she have problems enough?

GABRIEL: We play the hand as dealt. Maintain the pressure and exercise the killer instinct that brought you where you are today.

STEVIE: I didn't account for everything to be turned on it's head in an afternoon.

MARK: We always knew where we stood in council accommodation. (Beat) In council accommodation.

LAWRENCE: (Shaking his head) I don't think can close this one . . .

GABRIEL: Don't flinch, Larry. Shut your eyes, you can smell the close from here.

STEVIE: You think getting pregnant would bind you to the father regardless.

PAUSE. **MARK** REGARDS **STEVIE**.

MARK: Regardless of what?

LAWRENCE: I can't do this to them.

GABRIEL: You never flinch, Lawrence. 'I've never flinched in my life'. Your words.

STEVIE: Ties that bind, isn't that what they say? Isn't that's what they tell you to believe?

MARK: Stevie?

GABRIEL: Close and kill, Larry. Close . . . and . . . *kill.*

LAWRENCE: For God's sake, you're talking about people not chickens . . .

MARK: Stevie?

PAUSE. **LAWRENCE** BREAKS TO A SPACE AWAY FROM **GABRIEL**. **GABRIEL** REGARDS **LAWRENCE**, THEN TAKES OUT A MOBILE TELEPHONE FROM HIS JACKET.

GABRIEL: What's your home number again, Lawrence? Ah, yes.

GABRIEL DIALS.

LAWRENCE: What're you doing?

GABRIEL: I just thought your wife could have that umbrella waiting for your arrival home this evening. In the event of a blizzard . . . (Into 'phone) Hello?

LAWRENCE: How dare you! Hang up! Hang up that 'phone! How dare you!

LAWRENCE ADVANCES ON **GABRIEL**, BUT **GABRIEL** HOLDS HIM AT BAY.

GABRIEL: (Into 'phone) Hello sweetheart, it's daddy. (Pause) I miss you too baby. Is mummy there? (Pause) Okay. (Pause) Okay. (Pause) Well you tell mummy-in-the-bath that daddy-in-the-suit will be coming home around seven o'clock. (Pause) Seven. (Pause) Seven o'clock. (Pause) Well sweetheart that depends. Have you finished reading your school book? Well, finish reading your school book and we'll see about that. (Pause) Yes, I might bring you something. Yes, it might be something you'll like. (Pause) And Daddy loves you sweetheart. (Smiling) And not really to you too baby. (Hangs up)

GABRIEL SMILES AT **LAWRENCE**. PAUSE.

LAWRENCE: That was . . . that was fucking lousy.

GABRIEL: Simply trying to re-ignite your motivation, Larry.

LAWRENCE: Jesus Christ Almighty . . .

GABRIEL: Keep your dependants to the fore and you'll *never* fall prey to self-indulgence.

LAWRENCE: A line of haema-pericardium runs in my family for God's sake.

GABRIEL: (Turning to **MARK'S** two prints and regarding them) My baby'd love a set of these.

LAWRENCE: If the sac round my heart's filling with blood as we speak I shudder to think what I'll be dealing with a month from now.

GABRIEL SMILES AT **LAWRENCE**, AND TAKES THE PICTURES OFF THE MANTELPIECE.

IN THE KITCHEN **STEVIE** REACHES FORWARD AND PICKS UP THE PIECE OF PAPER WRITTEN ON BY **LAWRENCE**. SHE UNFOLDS AND READS IT. SHE STARTS TO LAUGH.

MARK: What's so funny?

STEVIE SLIDES THE PIECE OF PAPER ACROSS THE TABLE TO **MARK**. **GABRIEL** ENTERS THE KITCHEN CARRYING THE TWO ANIMAL PRINTS.

GABRIEL: We were in the other room admiring your work, and I was wondering how much you'd ask for the pair?

MARK: Nothing.

GABRIEL: Great.

MARK: No. Sorry. They're not for sale.

GABRIEL: Can't I make you an offer? My little girl would just love these.

MARK: I can't release individual prints.

GABRIEL: I don't want – Look. It's really no big deal. Just these.

LAWRENCE: (Entering) Mark gave you his answer, Gabriel. Now drop it.

GABRIEL GLARES AT **LAWRENCE**, BUT HE STANDS HIS GROUND. PAUSE.

GABRIEL: Sorry Mr D.

LAWRENCE: (Turning to **MARK** and **STEVIE**) You've seen the cost of the treatment?

STEVIE: Yes.

LAWRENCE: So what do you think?

STEVIE: What do I think? I think it's laughable.

LAWRENCE: Really?

STEVIE: I laughed, so it must be.

LAWRENCE: Speaking personally, I think it's fantastic value. And I'm here to tell you this price can only stand for twenty eight days.

MARK: What happens after twenty-eight days?

LAWRENCE: The price must increase.

MARK: Why?

LAWRENCE: Afraid I can't say.

STEVIE: Why not?

LAWRENCE: It's beyond our remit.

MARK: How far does your remit extend?

LAWRENCE: Not that far. It's a complex business. This is a special offer as we're new to the area. Our prices are being artificially suppressed to make it as easy as possible for you to secure your property.

STEVIE: If you'd told us the price when I originally asked you'd've saved yourself a ton of trouble.

LAWRENCE: It's no trouble.

STEVIE: We've really wasted your time I'm afraid.

LAWRENCE: Don't be afraid. Our time is your time.

STEVIE: Even if we agreed our walls required urgent treatment –

MARK: I'm certainly not half as confident now as before . . .

LAWRENCE: Not *if* you agreed, Stevie. Some things are incontrovertible. They are the incontrovertible things.

STEVIE: (Holding the piece of paper) Look around. Look at us. Do we look like we have this kind of money?

LAWRENCE: My dear, few do. I take it you're familiar with the term *credit arrangement*.

MARK: We don't believe in credit.

LAWRENCE: You've got a mortgage.

STEVIE: That's different. It's – a mortgage is just different.

GABRIEL: Think of it as a necessary extension to your mortgage.

LAWRENCE: You can afford the treatment, Stevie. It's as simple as that.

STEVIE: No, we can't.

LAWRENCE: Yes you can. It's that simple.

STEVIE: No. We don't have the money. Don't you see? There's no point continuing any longer because we simply can't afford to buy.

LAWRENCE: You can afford the treatment, Stevie. Because we can bend over backwards to make it affordable.

MARK: If they can bend over backwards maybe we *can* afford it.

LAWRENCE: That's the spirit. Be positive.

STEVIE: Mark. Shut up.

GABRIEL: The glass is always half full, never half empty.

MARK: I know you think I'm being weak now, Steve. I know you think I'm betraying our original intentions. But this is in reality so *un*-weak. The admission of sensible doubt, Steve . . . the strength to reach out and listen to the helping hand for the good of my family –

STEVIE: Shut the fuck up, Marky. Please. Now. Just shut the f – (Beat) Please. (Pause) (To **GABRIEL** AND **LAWRENCE**) Now listen to me. You have to listen to me now because we don't have any money and you're much, *much* better at this than we are. What I'm saying – you see how we are. We're nothing special. We're not out of the ordinary – just trying to deal with each new thing as it hits us, like everyone else. But we can't deal with this. We don't know how to deal with you . . . and *this*. We don't know *business*. We don't know what to do. We don't know how to stop this. You've seen it all a hundred times and you twist every word to your advantage. It's your job, I know, and you're – believe me – you are *very* good at it. But you've got to stop now because I don't know what happens if you get us to sign. We've got no money. I'm sorry, but we just haven't got any money. We have *no* money. I wish we did. I know you say we don't need money, but that's not true. I know, at least, that's not *actually* true. Sooner or later we have to have the money, and if we missed payments you go to court and we could lose our home. So please. I'm asking you to help us. Things aren't exactly easy for us at the moment. You've probably noticed. So you must appreciate how unfair this is – how one-sided this is. So I'm asking you to stop now. I know it's not what you want, but as one human-being to another. Please. Stop this now and leave us be.

PAUSE.

GABRIEL: We can't stop now. You know that. (Beat) Not with your house in such an appalling condition. It would be irresponsibility bordering on the criminal.

STEVIE: No. Listen to what I'm saying –

GABRIEL: Providing we remain within the limits of contract law, Stevie, you'll be pleasantly surprised what's possible. May I ask what the monthly income is for the house?

STEVIE: Please stop.

GABRIEL: The monthly income is what, Mark?

STEVIE: Please. Go!

MARK: She makes thirteen hundred a month.

STEVIE: Don't tell them anything. If we don't tell them anything they have no reason to stay.

GABRIEL: Plain old-fashioned panic, Mark. Just like we said.

MARK: Thirteen hundred a month, after tax.

STEVIE: Get out of my house.

GABRIEL: (Writing it down) All personal details treated in the strictest confidence, of course.

STEVIE: Oh Christ . . . *Mark*? *Do* something!

MARK: What helps them now could help us later.

STEVIE: It's just a loan Marky! There's nothing wrong with our walls, they just want to hook us up to a blue whale of a loan!

GABRIEL: Shall we crack on, Mr D? (Pause) The sooner we finish the sooner you can get home to your wife. I expect she's expecting you.

AFTER A MOMENT **LAWRENCE** RESIGNEDLY TAKES THE PEN AND PAPER FROM **GABRIEL**.

LAWRENCE: (Writing on the paper) I am now writing down how little the treatment will cost per month under our terms of credit.

STEVIE: No! We have *no* money.

LAWRENCE OFFERS THE PAPER TO **MARK**, WHO TAKES IT. **MARK** READS.

LAWRENCE: All interest fully inclusive. Naturally.

GABRIEL: Surprisingly low, isn't it?

STEVIE: We can't afford it.

GABRIEL: You haven't looked.

STEVIE: We can't afford anything.

LAWRENCE: It's irresistible. I'm sure Mark agrees with me.

MARK: I . . . I . . . no. Actually, I'm sorry. I don't think we can afford this.

STEVIE: At last! At last you're here!

LAWRENCE: But that represents tremendous value.

STEVIE: We can't afford *anything*.

LAWRENCE: Whichever way you look at it, that represents *phenomenal* value.

STEVIE: We can't afford –

LAWRENCE: (Cutting in) *Okay*! (He stands) (Pause) Okay. (Pause) You can't afford anything. I heard you the first time. You said it and I heard it. Okay. (Beat) Now here's something that'll wipe the sour from your face, Stevie. Just listen to this – I don't know if it's possible 'cause we don't normally do this so early in the promotion. I haven't looked into the precedent. Precedent may well rule this out, though I'm 90% certain it won't. And this has to be strictly *entre nous*, you understand.

GABRIEL: If your neighbours get wind of the offer Mr Davidson's about to make, well, we've seen poison put down for a pair of Siamese kittens over less.

MARK: We don't have any kittens.

GABRIEL: A taller fence between you and next door might nevertheless be advisable. Money can be a great source of division. I've personally seen an electric heater thrown into a well-stocked goldfish pond. I even witnessed a dog with it's tongue stapled to it's cheek in money-envy. Human nature at it's very worst. And once again it's the pets who take the brunt.

LAWRENCE: To favoured clients we would pay – now listen closely. To erect an advertising board outside your house we would pay two hundred pounds a week for ten weeks.

GABRIEL: That's two thousand pounds.

LAWRENCE: Assuming you fall into the appropriate category.

GABRIEL: Two thousand pounds.

MARK: What if we don't fall into the appropriate category?

LAWRENCE: Think positive.

GABRIEL: Two thousand pounds.

MARK: Cash?

LAWRENCE: Cash? (Pause) Not quite cash exactly.

MARK: Not cash.

LAWRENCE: Not in the strict understanding of the word 'cash'.

GABRIEL: Two thousand pounds in the form of a deduction from the total treatment cost.

STEVIE: A deduction?

LAWRENCE: (Writing on the piece of paper) Bringing the treatment cost *right down* to . . .

LAWRENCE PUSHES THE PAPER TOWARDS **MARK**. PAUSE.

MARK: This is per month?

LAWRENCE: I want your word you won't tell your neighbours. I can't have the safety of any animals you may acquire in the future on my conscience. The neighbours get wind of this they tell the whole street, and I'll be trampled underfoot in the rush to stampede.

MARK: (Showing the paper to **STEVIE**) Stevie, it's significantly less than the original figure.

GABRIEL: A whole *two thousand* pounds less.

LAWRENCE: *Plus*, should the board prove a success we'd be in a position to extend its duration of display.

MARK: For how long?

STEVIE: It doesn't matter how long, Mark –

MARK: For how much?

STEVIE: It doesn't matter how much –

LAWRENCE: Another thousand.

MARK: Pounds?

LAWRENCE: Very probably. And I'm still being conservative.

MARK: Shit, Stevie. We should really start thinking about this.

STEVIE: Marky, forget them. Think of the baby.

MARK: They're knocking off *three thousand pounds*!

STEVIE: Don't you see what they're doing?

LAWRENCE: I can't understand what your problem is. After all I've slashed from the price I don't understand why you still have that expression on your face.

STEVIE: You understand what the problem is. You know what the problem is because I keep telling you what the problem is. We do not have –

LAWRENCE: If I had a pound for everyone who told me they hadn't a penny I'd be leaning over a balcony overlooking the Atlantic right now – chilled wine in one hand, grilled sardine in the other. (Turning away from the table) All right. All right. (He sighs) You're a young couple. Much like my own daughter and son-in-law, except you speak to me. You're struggling to make your way . . . new-born in production, which won't be easy. Trust me, I understand.

STEVIE: If you understand then go.

LAWRENCE: (He glances at **GABRIEL** then sits) This doesn't pass beyond this kitchen.

GABRIEL: You're the boss.

LAWRENCE: I want your word.

GABRIEL: Which one?

LAWRENCE: Of honour.

GABRIEL: You've got it.

LAWRENCE: I've got it?

GABRIEL: It's yours.

LAWRENCE: This gets round the office, I'm a laughing stock of grotesque proportions.

GABRIEL: As God is my witness.

LAWRENCE: Which he is.

GABRIEL: I believe it.

LAWRENCE: You should.

GABRIEL: I do.

LAWRENCE: Then let's do this quickly now. (Leaning towards **MARK** and **STEVIE**) Application of the full treatment to a house generally takes between three to four days. But the majority of our clients prefer work to start at the beginning of the week. It's a cultural idiosyncrasy. In Scandinavia they prefer you to start a job Sunday evening, but that's the Arctic winter for you.

STEVIE: Are you deaf?

MARK: Let him finish.

LAWRENCE: So the lads start Monday finish late Wednesday, early Thursday. Can't begin the next job until the following Monday, but they're still on the payroll over Thursday and Friday. Paying them for doing what?

GABRIEL: Nothing.

LAWRENCE: Even less than that. I'll be blunt. I'm prepared to give you money it would otherwise cost to keep our technicians fannying around if, *if* you'd be prepared to have them start the urgently needed treatment of your house in the middle of a week. (To **GABRIEL**) You, of course, didn't hear this.

GABRIEL: My ears are abuzz with silence.

MARK: How much is that worth?

LAWRENCE: In cash terms –

GABRIEL: Though cash would be represented in the form of a further deduction form the total treatment cost.

LAWRENCE: I'd estimate somewhere between five to six hundred pounds. And that's very conservative.

MARK: Another six hundred off?

LAWRENCE: Utter this to another living soul and I deny we've even met.

MARK: That's a discount of over three thousand pounds!

STEVIE: Do you really not see what's happening here?

LAWRENCE: Let Gabriel have a set of these wonderful pictures and you can lose another one-fifty from what's left of the price.

MARK: I mean I'd love to. But I have to consider the project as a complete entity. If prints fell into circulation the currency of the book would be devalued. A key element of my strategy is that of surprise.

STEVIE: (Standing) Okay that's enough. Now get out.

LAWRENCE: Throw in a set for my wife and make it three hundred.

MARK: Three hundred?

LAWRENCE: Four fifty if you run off a pair for the office. Brighten the place up. But stop me now. If I continue any longer my name ends up in a Christmas cracker. I don't think there's been an offer this low in the history of the company.

MARK: Can we think about it?

STEVIE: There is nothing to think about!

LAWRENCE: I'd personally love you to think about it, Mark. I'd personally give you all the time in the world to think about it. I think thinking time is not only useful but essential. You need time to think and in an ideal world you should have as much thinking time as you need. Unfortunately, however, this is the final day of the promotion. I'm sorry, but there it is.

MARK: Oh.

STEVIE: (Advancing on Lawrence) No, no . . . hang on. Just hang on one second. A minute ago you said it was *early* in the promotion. You said, 'we don't normally do this so early in the promotion'. That's what you said. How can it be early in the promotion and the *final day* of the promotion at the same time?

LAWRENCE: (Beat) That's what I said, yes. But, well, yes, no, that's what I said . . .

STEVIE: That's *exactly* what you said! See, Mark: *liars!* They're lying. They're making this up from one second to the next!

GABRIEL: The final day of the promotion *on this street.*

PAUSE.

STEVIE: What?

GABRIEL: It's a street by street promotion. The promotion in its entirety is indeed, in its early stages. But the promotion on this street expires at six o'clock tonight. It then moves to another street. They're very strict about this. The promotion is executed like this in the interest of equity. We can't make a general offer to everyone at the same time as this wouldn't be an offer in the accepted sense. This would merely be the same as a shoe shop advertising a sale three hundred and sixty five days a year, year in year out. Which is a deceit. Legal. But deceitful. That's not how we like to play. We like to play cricket, and we do not like to tamper with the ball. In this, I have to say, we're exceptional. The general trend is for standards to fall – you've no doubt noticed. Most don't, because expectations are falling even faster than standards. As long as this persists society will continue to shuffle mutely towards the sewer. Which is an outcome Ex-Cote will not accept lightly. (Pause) So this is, I'm proud to say, the final day of the promotion as far as you're concerned.

MARK: Shit.

GABRIEL: Believe me, we're as disappointed for you as must be for yourselves. However.

STEVIE: Marky, it's *bullshit.*

MARK: It's a discount of over four thousand pounds! We've got to strike while the iron's hot.

STEVIE: It's total fabrication. They want us to buy into a loan it'll take twenty years to pay off – at a rate of interest paying them twice the actual cost of the treatment.

MARK: It's our home, Stevie – we can find the money!

STEVIE: How? *How*? I only just scrape the mortgage as it is. And then there's the baby –

MARK: Don't you understand? It's the baby I'm thinking of.

GABRIEL: You're a family man now, Mark. Think of the baby. Protect it with Ex-Cote.

MARK: (To **STEVIE**) How can you think I'm not thinking of the baby? Fuck it, Steve . . . *who do you think my book is for*?

PAUSE.

STEVIE: Oh God.

GABRIEL: (Taking a formal-looking document from a briefcase) What time did you say you had to see Mr Arnold, Mr Davidson?

LAWRENCE: (Looking at his watch) I can keep him waiting twenty minutes at most.

GABRIEL: This is a contract. (Offers it to **MARK**) If you'd like to cast an eye over it you'll find everything clearly laid out.

STEVIE: (Suddenly scared) Marky, don't touch that.

LAWRENCE: Exact terms of your loan to be written-in, of course.

MARK TAKES THE FORM.

STEVIE: Don't look at it.

MARK: (Waving her away and reading over the contract) I'm trying to concentrate.

STEVIE: My salary can't support anything more.

MARK: I know – don't you ever stop *nagging*?

STEVIE: If you know, tell me how you can even look at that?

MARK: Don't you understand *anything*? The book, of course.

STEVIE: What do you mean *the book*?

MARK: My book. We'll pay for Ex-Cote with the income from my book.

PAUSE.

STEVIE: Income from *what book*, Mark? You've done two out of twenty six pictures, and one of those is completely inappropriate. What book?

MARK: Money will be no object 'cause my book will blow toddlers heads off. Gabriel should know.

STEVIE: Gabriel?

MARK: He's got a toddler, and he said he hasn't seen anything to touch what I've done.

GABRIEL: Nothing anywhere.

STEVIE: Are you seriously suggesting we lock ourselves into a twenty year loan for a five figure sum on the basis of 'A' is for armadillo?

MARK: Not just the armadillo, Stevie. And 'B' is for bunny.

STEVIE: What do you mean *and 'B' is for bunny*? Bunny doesn't work, Mark. You agreed.

MARK: I bet you can't guess what 'C' is for.

STEVIE: We agreed 'B' is for bunny didn't cut the mustard.

GABRIEL: We think 'B' is for bunny is extraordinary.

MARK: I listened to your comments, Steve. But Lawrence and Gabriel think 'B' is for bunny's brilliant.

STEVIE: Lawrence and Gabriel?

MARK: They think the bunny works brilliantly. I've been thinking about it and I think, on balance, I agree with them.

GABRIEL: We think the bunny's stunning.

PAUSE.

STEVIE: Marky . . . have you lost your fucking mind?

MARK: Work of distinction seldom lacks attention, Steve. That's a universal truth. You can't be too cut and dried where kids're concerned.

GABRIEL: They're a law unto themselves.

STEVIE: Oh you poor, stupid . . . *They* think the bunny works? Who the fuck are *they*?

MARK: They understand who I am, Stevie.

STEVIE: Marky. Listen to me. They know nothing about who you are, and even less about your book. Furthermore, they don't actually give a shit about either.

GABRIEL: We know talent when we see it. Don't we, Mr Davidson?

LAWRENCE: I don't know. I suppose . . .

GABRIEL: You can do better than that Mr D.

MARK: I like 'B' is for bunny, Stevie. And at the end of the day I have to be true to myself.

STEVIE: No, Mark. At this instant you have to be true to *me* and *the baby*.

GABRIEL: Your book will break all records, Mark. I confidently predict you'll pay off the loan within three months of publication.

STEVIE: You don't know him from Adam!

GABRIEL: Adam who?

82

MARK: They believe in me, Stevie. They believe in my book.

STEVIE: I believe in your book, Mark.

MARK: Do you?

STEVIE: If it's done properly, of *course* I do.

MARK: *Properly*? *Your* properly?

STEVIE: No, no. Mark. Please. I believe in you, Marky. But let's talk about this later, okay? Alone. Okay? Marky?

MARK: If you believe in my book let's sign the contract. If you believe in my book there's no reason why we can't sign.

STEVIE: Marky, please. Don't do this.

GABRIEL: Without mutual trust a relationship's like riding in tandem with just –

STEVIE: You said that!

GABRIEL: Some things bear repetition.

MARK: (To **LAWRENCE**) Have you got a pen?

STEVIE: Mark –

MARK: (To **LAWRENCE**) Give me a pen.

LAWRENCE: Don't you think we should all just calm down a minute before anyone starts signing things?

GABRIEL: (Pushing past Lawrence and offering his gold pen) Here you are, Mark.

MARK: Where do I sign?

STEVIE: Mark, you're not signing anything.

MARK: Show me where I sign.

GABRIEL: (Indicating) There, there, and there.

STEVIE SNATCHES UP THE CONTRACT AND TEARS IT IN HALF. SHE LETS THE TWO PIECES FALL TO THE FLOOR.

STEVIE: You're not signing anything.

PAUSE. **GABRIEL** THEN REACHES INTO HIS BRIEFCASE AND TAKES ANOTHER CONTRACT AND LAYS IT BEFORE **MARK**.

GABRIEL: (Indicating where to sign) There . . . there . . . and there.

STEVIE SIMPLY REACHES FORWARD AND PICKS UP THIS CONTRACT. SHE SLOWLY TEARS IT IN TWO. PAUSE.

GABRIEL: Stevie, who isn't afraid of commitment – financial or emotional? And yet we must nevertheless commit to things unknown in the hope that our fear will be overcome. Irrational fear, Stevie. We see it all the time. (Beat) I have another twenty contracts in this case, and forty more in the car. If Mark needs to do the right thing by his family, don't you think you should control yourself . . . (laying a third contract before **MARK**) . . . and let him?

MARK STARTS TO SIGN.

STEVIE: Without the signature of the joint-mortgage holder, that contract is worthless.

MARK: (Signing his name) One for the house. (Signing his name) One for the baby. (Signing his name) And one for us.

STEVIE: Without my signature it's worth less than used toilet paper.

MARK NOW HOLDS THE PEN OUT FOR **STEVIE**.

MARK: Now you.

LAWRENCE: I think we should all just take a long, deep breath, and just calm this right the way down.

MARK: (Holding out the pen) You believe in my book, Stevie. You just said so. So sign. Hey – we can crack open the champagne in a double celebration. (Crossing to the fridge and taking out the Champagne) To the book and the house!

STEVIE: You should've talked to me about the book, Mark. You should have talked to me about walking out of your job *before* you walked out.

MARK: It was a spur of the moment.

STEVIE: You walk off a job we needed on the spur of the moment. You turn down Angelo on the spur of the moment. You invite lowlife into my house on the spur of the moment.

GABRIEL: Lowlife?

STEVIE: You buy £50 bottles of champagne on the spur of a moment, and now you want to tie us to a loan we don't want and can't pay – all on the spur of yet another *stupid* moment. This isn't *college* anymore, Marky. I can't keep living on the spur of your moments. I'm pregnant. I need moments with less fucking spurs.

MARK: That's *our* house. Not your house. *Ours.*

STEVIE: What?

MARK: You said *my,* again.

STEVIE: Why not? Don't I pay for *everything*?

MARK: I need you to sign the contract, Stevie.

STEVIE: Never.

GABRIEL: Just sign it, Stevie.

STEVIE: As far as I'm concerned there are just two humans in this room.

MARK: I want you to sign the contract.

STEVIE: I wanted you to start on the nursery, *like you promised.* I wanted to go to self-defence. But mostly I want a life that doesn't keep coming at me out of the blue.

MARK: Sign it as a sign.

STEVIE: A sign? A sign of what?

MARK: Of your faith. In my book.

PAUSE. **STEVIE** SLOWLY PICKS UP THE TWO PRINTS AND TEARS THEM IN HALF. SHE THROWS THE PIECES ON THE TABLE BEFORE **MARK**.

STEVIE: That's how much faith I have in your book, Mark.

LAWRENCE: Maybe it's time we went, Mr James.

GABRIEL: ABC, Larry. ABC.

MARK: You complete bitch.

PAUSE. **MARK** PICKS UP THE PIECES OF HIS TWO PRINTS.

STEVIE: I'm sorry, Marky.

MARK: You're sorry?

STEVIE: I'm sorry.

PAUSE.

MARK: Show me how sorry.

STEVIE: What?

MARK: Come here, Stevie. (Beat) Please.

STEVIE CROSSES OVER TO **MARK**. HE REGARDS HER FOR A MOMENT AND STROKES HER HAIR.

STEVIE: I'm sorry, Marky.

MARK: I know, Stevie. (He strokes her face gently with his hand) I know. (He suddenly grabs a handful of her hair and pulls her head backwards) Now sign the contract and show me just how sorry you *really* are.

STEVIE: (In severe pain) Marky!

LAWRENCE: Mr James –

GABRIEL: Start packing, Larry.

STEVIE: You're tearing my hair out!

THE TWO SALESMEN START PACKING THEIR BAGS.

MARK: I should tear out your arms for what you just did. Now be sorry and sign.

STEVIE: No!

MARK: (He presses the struggling **STEVIE'S** head onto the contract on the table) Sign it sign it sign it sign it –

MARK SUDDENLY LETS OUT A LOUD CRY OF PAIN. IN THE STRUGGLE **STEVIE** HAS MANAGED TO GET A TIGHT GRIP ON MARKS GROIN. **MARK** FREEZES WITH PAIN AND LETS GO OF **STEVIE'S** HAIR. **STEVIE** IS NOW IN CONTROL AND HER GRIP TIGHTENS.

STEVIE: (Not shouted, but with absolute conviction) I . . . said . . . *no*.

STEVIE PUNCHES HER GRIPPING HAND HARD INTO **MARK'S** CROTCH, CAUSING HIM TO LET OUT AN AGONISED GROAN. **STEVIE** RELEASES HER GRIP. **MARK** STANDS IN SHOCK FOR A MOMENT, THEN FALLS TO HIS KNEES BEFORE **STEVIE** IN VOICE-PARALYSING AGONY. ONLY THE MOST STRAINED, CHOKED, GUTTURAL SOUND MANAGES TO EMERGE FROM HIS MOUTH.

PAUSE.

GABRIEL AND **LAWRENCE** FINISH PACKING. **MARK** SITS ON HIS HAUNCHES IN FRONT OF THE TABLE, ROCKING SLOWLY IN PAIN; HIS HANDS BURIED IN HIS CROTCH. ONLY **STEVIE** IS PERCEPTIBLY MOBILE, AS SHE RECOVERS FROM **MARK'S** ATTACK, LEANING ON THE TABLE FOR SUPPORT.

GABRIEL: Whatever you're paying for self-defence classes, I'd say it was money well spent.

STEVIE: Get out.

GABRIEL: (Packing) You know, it's people like your boyfriend who make my job a nightmare. Me? I'm a trained professional. I behave accordingly. I know what I want and how to get it. But *you* people. You're the worst. You have no self-discipline. You're rude, vague, and you utterly waste my time. You don't know what you need. You don't know what you want. You're a prick tease. You ask us back but come the moment of truth you plead poverty and scream blue murder. *This is my job.* This is what feeds my child.

STEVIE: Just get out.

GABRIEL STOPS AND REGARDS **STEVIE**. HE CROSSES TO HER. PAUSE.

GABRIEL: (Adopting a much gentler tone) Stevie. Look. I can tell you're upset. Emotions frequently run high, we see it a thousand times. It's perfectly natural. They mean far less than we credit, and at the end of the day shouldn't be allowed to obstruct us. Listen. No flim flam. No bullshit. You really should have your walls treated. If – and I speak now as a father myself – if only for the sake of the baby. Why don't you make us a nice cup of tea and we all sit down and work through your concerns from the top? Calmly and quietly. From the beginning. I'm sure if we all sit down in a spirit of calm –

STEVIE: Another word and I call the police.

PAUSE. **GABRIEL** ASSESSES THAT THE GAME IS FINALLY UP.

GABRIEL: It's your house. For as long as it remains standing. A final word of advice about your 'partner': I think you could do better.

STEVIE: Fuck off.

PAUSE. THE PACKING IS FINALLY COMPLETED.

GABRIEL: Can I drop you somewhere, Larry?

LAWRENCE: Aren't we going back to the office?

GABRIEL: I'm going back to the office, yes.

LAWRENCE: To see Mr Arnold.

GABRIEL: *I'm* going to see Arnold before he closes, yes.

LAWRENCE: You?

GABRIEL: That's right, Larry.

LAWRENCE: And me.

GABRIEL: No.

LAWRENCE: Not me?

GABRIEL: You flinched, Larry. I kept telling you not to, but you flinched. In this business the rule is simple: flinch and die.

LAWRENCE: But –

GABRIEL: No buts, Lawrence. I suspect, when you look back, you'll realise you should've stuck to chickens.

LAWRENCE: The fucking supertsores sent me under!

GABRIEL: I feel for you, Larry, I really do. But . . . and don't take this personally . . . I just don't have any more *time* for you. (Looks at his watch) Can I drop you somewhere or not?

LAWRENCE: (Dazed) What?

GABRIEL: Where can I drop you?

PAUSE.

LAWRENCE: Nowhere.

GABRIEL: Nowhere?

LAWRENCE: (Beat) I'll catch a bus.

GABRIEL: A bus? Do real people still use those? C'mon. Where can I drop you?

LAWRENCE: I will catch a bus.

BEAT.

GABRIEL: I understand. Take care of yourself, Lawrence.

GABRIEL PICKS UP ALL THE CASES AND LEAVES.
LAWRENCE REGARDS **STEVIE** AND **MARK**. PAUSE.

STEVIE: Get out of my house.

MARK: (Weakly from his position on the floor) *Our* . . . house . . .

LAWRENCE: Try and work this out. Work this out between you, 'cause now's no time to be alone. (Beat) I know whereof I speak. (Beat) I've got a theory about 'now' . . . and my theory about 'now' . . . (Pause) Nah. (Pause) Forget I ever opened my mouth. (Pause) I'm sorry. (Beat) What else can I say . . . except . . . (Beat) I mean . . . what else can I say to her?

LONG PAUSE. **LAWRENCE** SLOWLY TURNS AND LEAVES.
THE FRONT DOOR CLOSES.

SILENCE. **STEVIE** SLOWLY STANDS UPRIGHT. SHE SLOWLY
TURNS AND REGARDS **MARK**. HE IS BREATHING HARD.
LONG PAUSE. **STEVIE** CROSSES TO **MARK** AND STANDS
OVER HIM.

STEVIE: I'm gonna show you something, Marky. (Pause) I'm gonna
show you what to do when I'm at work and you're here by yourself and
there's a knock at the door. (She stoops and grabs him under an armpit
and starts to drag him towards the back door) You're them . . . I'm you.

MARK WHIMPERS AS HE IS HELPED/DRAGGED TO THE
BACK DOOR. **STEVIE** OPENS THE BACK DOOR AND PULLS
MARK OUTSIDE. SHE THEN RETURNS INTO THE KITCHEN
AND CLOSES THE DOOR ON **MARK**.

STEVIE: (Calling out) Knock on the door. (Pause) Knock on the door,
Marky.

MARK KNOCKS THREE TIMES ON THE DOOR. **STEVIE**
HESITATES FOR A MOMENT, THEN OPENS THE DOOR.

STEVIE: (Formally) Yes? (Pause) Say it. (Pause) *Say it.*

MARK: (Weakly) I wonder if you . . . (Pause) I wonder if you . . .
(Pause) I wonder if –

STEVIE: 'Not . . . today . . . thank . . . you'.

STEVIE CLOSES THEN BOLTS THE DOOR. SHE STANDS WITH
HER BACK AGAINST IT. SHE TAKES A DEEP BREATH AND
EXHALES.

MARK STARTS TO KNOCK QUIETLY ON THE DOOR. **STEVIE**
DOESN'T MOVE. **MARK** KNOCKS AGAIN, BUT **STEVIE** STILL
DOES NOT MOVE. AS THE KNOCKING BECOMES LOUD AND
INSISTENT, **STEVIE** SLOWLY SLIDES DOWN THE DOOR AND
CROUCHES AGAINST ITS BASE. **MARK** NOW BANGS
URGENTLY ON THE DOOR AS **STEVIE** WRAPS BOTH ARMS
PROTECTIVELY AROUND HER BELLY. THE BANGING
CONTINUES. **STEVIE** FINALLY PUTS ONE HAND ON THE
DOOR HANDLE AS THE LIGHTS SLOWLY FADE. THE
BANGING CONTINUES . . .

BLACKOUT.